FAST

FOOD

<u>*And Other Social Dilemmas*</u>

*Workplace Symptoms of the African-American Family
Breakdown*

TABLE OF CONTENTS

FOREWORD

What explains the current general social-economic state of blacks in America and in the job market specifically? Can we look at some alarming trends and truths in the job market and get real insights as to what has happened to cause or continue them? The dilemma; Do African-Americans remain victims of an oppressive white ruling class or have we become our own worst enemy?

When I began this book in 2006 and completed it in 2007 the national unemployment rate according to the U.S. Bureau of Labor Statistics hovered around 4.7 percent. Today it has at times more than doubled that number. According to BLS statistics the seasonally adjusted January 2012 unemployment rate for African American youths, the primary focus of this book, was 38.5%. Compare this to Hispanic youths at 24.9% and White youths at 21.1% over the same period. This is not a political statement. I mention it for the simple reason of providing accurate context so that some don't get the idea that I am ignoring the currently difficult job market when I make certain points and cover various topics.

Though I am acutely aware of the current job climate, I believe that the major tenets presented and discussed in this volume remain applicable today without qualification. African-Americans remain the least compensated in the job market, with the lowest per capita earnings even compared to Hispanics who have made significant gains over the past decade. According to BLS Blacks also remain low in the number of those promoted to managerial and executive positions in the labor force.

Most assuredly some of this is due to covert discriminatory practices that one can do little to address except continue to try and persuade individuals at the heart level. However much of these seeming inequities I believe are the direct results of the social issues addressed in this book that have just done what any good pathogen does. It spreads from one domain of our lives to others. If for instance you acquire a physical health problem that you fail to address properly, it will surely affect you psychologically due to the ensuing mental stress. Likewise if you fail to resolve some life issue that is affecting you mentally the stress involved in this may develop into physical problems as stress tends to localize in our bodies. Disease or pathologies rarely rest. They tend to be very busy, often crossing our most carefully constructed boundaries and they tend to consume.

My concern is how these pathologies, these social dilemmas if you will, show up in the world or domain of work. How they tend to leave many blacks only prepared for lower paid employment. And it is fair to say that if they are not properly addressed the unemployment rates will only matter in terms of the amount of job openings available. If and when rates decrease they will still not affect what kinds of jobs African-Americans are qualified to do and I see no evidence that they will affect performance once in those positions available to them. In many cases the problems started long before the first job application. Those problems are what this book is about and they have not gone away due to higher unemployment rates. In all likelihood they have only been exacerbated by them.

Fast Food

INTRODUCTION

This book is primarily about a workplace symptom that is indicative of far greater underlying social problems. Keep that in mind. The workplace itself is not the problem, only one of many places where these symptoms manifest themselves.

It must also be said that when I began this book and formulated my opinions, it was not with the intent of hurting anyone's feelings or to dissuade anyone from seeking and maintaining honest employment. We all have the responsibility to, as near as possible, take care of our obligations and ourselves. And ideally no one who strives for excellence in the context of honest employment should be ashamed or embarrassed by what they do for a living. I believe wholeheartedly that excellence is the main quality to be desired and pursued in our vocations however humble, and is intrinsic to the worker, not the type of work. There's no less excellence to be found in foodservice, the main vocational focus of this exposition, than there is to be found in neurology. Someone can excel in hotel housekeeping as well as one can excel in quantum physics. That being said, there are definitely occupations, mainly those that require extensive training

to enter, that promotes, support, and reward excellence far more than do others. By their very nature they are usually higher paid. And higher paid occupations tend to offer more alternatives when establishing short and long-term life goals.

Yet I am keenly aware that there are those who believe and hold dearly to the notion that it doesn't matter what a person does for a living as long as it's honest employment. If you are someone who believes this I suggest a note of caution. If you continue to read this book it may change your mind or challenge your views dramatically. And change, or even the notion of change, can be very uncomfortable for many. There is still ample time however to stay sheltered and unchanged by what I see as a problem of astounding proportion. A problem that is indicative and illustrative of social issues most people avoid openly discussing for fear of sounding judgmental or worse. For when truth is spoken most times someone will be offended. This is probably unavoidable. Yet I have attempted to approach this work empathetically while remaining factual and open. And it is within the context of this openness that I also hope to begin to solicit the ideas and actions of needed change.

****

In most of the more densely populated areas of the country, African American males occupy a very large portion of the labor pool for the Foodservice Industry. As a vocational counselor I have administered hundreds and possibly thousands of career interest inventories to African American males with lengthy terms of foodservice employment. An interest inventory is a questionnaire that determines your best career choices based on your levels of interest. And I can attest that the majority of them showed that their career interests were mainly in the areas of science, technology, and the professions. Why then the inconsistency? Why this vast gap in between what appears to really get someone's juices going occupationally and what he is actually doing vocationally, often with no realistic plans of ever doing anything else? And why is this inconsistency so pervasive for this particular segment of the American workforce?

The inordinate and disproportional representation of African Americans in the lower echelons of the Foodservice Industry, particularly African American males, became a personal concern of mine long before it became a professional one as I am both African American and male. So I delve into this occupational and social phenomenon from multiple perspectives, the economic implications and general tenor of our nation not the least among them.

I state or imply no moral authority here. That is beneath the purpose of this work. My family has also been touched by many of the social maladies that we will delve into as we progress through these coming pages. But I have still attempted to take on these issues in an effort to help right us from (what I can see as) a course that is certainly genocidal on so many different planes.

****

There was a time in our evolution as a nation and a workforce when blacks were in positions of forced servitude as property. When after much political and military resistance the status of property was lifted, African Americans were then, due to overt discriminatory practices in education and the job market, forced to work mainly personal services and unskilled labor type positions. Basically performing many of the same tasks they had performed under sanctioned slavery, only now for barley livable wages. Today after the enactment of anti-discrimination laws in education and employment, and after viable entries into the middle and upper middle classes by many African Americans, why the continued saturation of these lower paid positions by those from the same ethnic group?

There are both credible and not so credible reasons for this. The credible reasons and opinions will be addressed over the remainder of this book. The "not so credible" reasons for this will be addressed now. They are not beliefs that are discussed as openly as they use to be, but it has been my experience that they are still the views held many.

I will not address them because I think they have merit or credence, but because on some level we are all indoctrinated. That is, we are the products of our environments in regards to certain

7

beliefs, prejudices, and stereotypes. We often believe what we have been told about someone else for no other reason than that we esteem the teller. We will do this with little or no direct experience of that person ourselves. We also tend to view and interpret whatever actual experiences we may have with that individual through the prism of our ideas that again have been influenced, to some degree, by the teller. This can be a safety measure for our protection. For instance, when we are small children and our parents say, "Don't talk to strangers." It can also border on or become pathology when skewed negatively. One example of this skewing could manifest itself for instance by us allowing certain negative behaviors by those in our social circles to be tolerated or completely ignored, while we intensely scrutinize and are critical of these same behaviors when displayed by those outside of our social circles. At best this is form of self-righteousness and at worst a form of group or collective narcissism.

The following are the two most presumptive and less credible arguments I have heard in our society that explains this phenomenon of blacks in lower paid vocational positions such as the ones we are discussing. I fear these arguments are consciously or subconsciously rooted in many more minds than will be admitted to. These popular arguments originate from two different parts of the human psyche, affect and spirituality. And even though most individuals would verbalize them only in the most closed of settings, as your author and guide I must first openly acknowledge that they exist. And also admit that I would prefer that they were not hanging around just below the surface of our thought process while investigating the remainder of this book. The first argument is that of *intellectual Incapability*. The second is that of a *biblical racial curse*.

****

The *intellectual incapability* argument is an argument of the affect (emotions) not an argument of the intellect (logic) because it is not logical. There is far too much empirical data to support just the opposite. To begin, when blacks were allowed by law to be considered property, most of the actual enslavement of African Americans occurred in southeastern states. In those states the general consensus that allowed free individuals of conscience to participate in this forced servitude was that lower cast blacks were not able to learn the basics of education, and as such had to be "taken care of" by their intellectual superiors. This argument was flawed and nonsensical on its face because in those very states there were actually restrictions forbidding the teaching of blacks to read and write. But if the capacity to learn was not there, why were the restrictions forbidding teaching needed? This argument would also over time be refuted at every level of occupational learning: semi-skilled, skilled, professional, and scientist, as restrictions were lessened and blacks entered careers in these occupational levels mastering their associated competencies.

All viable studies that I have read researching the causation for the differences in academic achievement scores of black students and white students have found that the primary factor is socio-economics.

This however is not a covert attempt to garner more funds for the educational system in this nation. Since the early sixties state and federal educational funding in America as a whole has increased annually. While it can be argued that some schools receive less than their fair or needed share, as a nation we spend on average three times more per child in the educational system today than we did in 1970. But since 1970 test scores for American school children have declined consistently.

And while the schools may share a portion of the responsibility for this decline, sound education in this nation has always been a collaboration of teachers and parents. So when parental examples, guidance, and participation is missing it stands to reason that parents, or a lack of parental involvement, is at the root of the other portion of this huge and threatening problem.

So it is not the economic solvency of the schools that these studies refer to. But the social and economic conditions of the homes of most black children (the majority of them being from single parent household) in comparison to those of most white children (with the majority of them being from two parent households with larger incomes).

Concerning the idea of a curse of biblical proportion that dictates blacks become the servants of whites and others. And please, even if you have no such biblical beliefs stay with us. There are those that do, and you may find it possible heretofore to intellectually address this argument in a systematic and logical way should the need ever arrive. None of us live in a vacuum. And you never know what genies will be loosed in the arena of frank and open discussion.

The Bible connects all post diluvium (*lat.* flood) families to the three sons of Noah: Ham, Shem, and Japheth. Ham was the youngest of the brothers. The curse occurred in Genesis 9:25-27. It took place because one day when Noah was intoxicated in his tent, "…Ham, the father of Canaan, saw the nakedness of his father, and told his two brothers without." (KJV) The other brothers wisely backed into the tent and covered their father. Noah was angry and placed a curse not on Ham but one of his sons, Canaan the father of the Canaanites and other civilizations. This child may have been the favorite or eldest of Ham his father. Who knows? If the curse had been placed on Ham the entire line would have been cursed. This is much like the curse in the royal branch of the Davidic line. It is commonly accepted that the curse was applied to King Jeconiah and his descendents (Jeremiah 22:30) and not applied to David's other son's, just those who were direct heirs to the throne.

Sons of Ham settled not only Canaan but also Babylon, Ethiopia, Egypt, Nineveh and other nations. God described Nebuchadnezzar, king of Babylon during the Jewish captivity, in Daniel's apocalyptic dream as the "head of gold. Daniel 2:37-39 *"37Thou, O king, art a king of kings: for the God of heaven hath given thee a kingdom, power, and strength, and glory. 38And wheresoever the children of men dwell, the beasts of the field and the fowls of the heaven hath he given into thine hand, and hath made thee ruler over them all. Thou art this head of gold. 39And after thee shall arise another kingdom inferior to thee,..."* (KJV) Every other empire after Nebuchadnezzar was depicted as a metal lesser in value and nobility. Egyptian science had calculated accurately the distance to the sun thousands of years before western science. They had developed unprecedented embalming and surgical techniques and possibly had discovered and utilized electricity. Not to make mention of their construction technology. Ethiopia was one of the wealthiest nations on earth during the time of Solomon's reign. Its ruler at that time, The Queen of Sheba, had a very close relationship with King Solomon. Some modern revisionists have attempted to relegate this relationship to something very platonic and benign. Yet Hebrew and Ethiopian tradition along with many historians believe that she and Solomon had a son. This royal lineage was claimed, recognized, and continued to the nation's most prominent modern day ruler, Emperor Haile Silassie, who essentially was the country's recognized monarch from 1916 to 1974.

These great civilizations have obviously declined in our time. But thousands of years from now the civilizations of our day will have probably declined and many disappeared. And none of us can say with any degree of accuracy what will be the conditions of the descendants of those once great civilizations at that time. I make no claims of being an anthropologist by any means. But with limited vicarious knowledge I have come to believe that this is the way of nations and civilizations. They rise and they fall. All have their triumphs and their failures. This is probably the one precept of uniformitarianism (the belief that all things pretty much continue as they have from the beginning) that I accept.

****

One last item before we get started in earnest. This book is well researched for quoted facts and statistical data. However, by and large it is a composite of my professional and personal opinions concerning the genesis of an observable phenomenon. Feel free to agree or disagree. If you believe differently, make your case and I will listen. I will make my email address available later.

CHAPTER I
The Family and Micro-Social Aspects

A Split Vision

      In our search for answers we will begin at the beginning - with the micro *family social unit*, which is largely accepted as the *prime building block* of macro-society. And we must come to grips with the reality that we live in rapidly changing times. Times my father could not imagine just one short generation ago. In his times, there existed unquestioned absolutes that provided for boundaries and accountability. In our times absolutes are fading and generating questions on even the nature of family itself. How is it defined? Who defines it? Does it have real meaning or impact in our very real workaday world? Or are we only dealing with, as many believe, simply an abstract concept that is mere smoke, mirrors, and words to satisfy an outdated ideal?

      In a free republic and the arena of ideas that has it's origins in that freedom there may be worthy debate concerning many of these questions. But time and focus will not allow for such debates in this book. So for the sake of discussion let us go with common consent here and stipulate that most peoples worldwide still view family as a father, mother, and siblings. If you share a different definition this book is not out to convert you. I would just like us to examine some of the positive reinforcements that we receive from this fundamentally accepted social system, whatever one chooses to label it. I would also like us to extrapolate or draw out some conclusions as to what happens when that unit functions in a way that fails to produce and provide those reinforcements.

      On balance, and speaking as a parent myself, let us also stipulate that just because proper social components such as work ethic, boundaries, accountability etc. are provided doesn't mean that they will always be accepted by each person in that family social unit or *"family of origin."* This is the family social unit in which you experience your formative years (infancy, early childhood, and childhood). Consequently, we will also look later on at this aspect of *"Rejected Social Tenets."* **(Most of us will naturally experiment with the moral and intellectual teachings of the family social unit of our youth, only to later return to that very same family of origin value system with many of us actually becoming very similar to our parents. However some of us never return to that value system but permanently reject all or most of it based on a variety of reasons.)**

***

Contemporary African American family social units are split very unevenly between traditional and single parent households, with single parent households not only outnumbering traditional households but also increasing at a much faster rate. What is gained from the traditional family setting and conversely what, if anything, is lost in the non-traditional setting is a very serious and underrated matter worthy of far more attention and action. For if we act on the premise that the family unit is the basic cell in the body of society, then the makeup of those cells truly matters. Just as in the human body the majority of individual cells must operate properly if the body is to be considered healthy, so it is with society at large and the individual households that make up that society.

Within the context of the family unit I believe the first thing necessary to our investigation is the examining parental roles, as parents are the ones that we charge with primary responsibility for the care and upbringing of their children. They are also the ones who physically initiate conception and gestation. The physical family begins with them. Further and more specifically we will first examine the role of fathers. This seems appropriate not because the role of fathers are any more important than the role of mothers, but because it's the role of father that is most often missing from the type family unit our attention will be focused on.

How important is this and why, is one matter we will be seeking to determine.

What Non-Abusive Fathers Bring To The Unit

I was recently told of one famous Hall of Fame football player, who himself grew up in a single parent household without his father and now heads an outreach program that works with men who are currently incarcerated. It is said that when visiting prisons to speak with these inmate groups, one of the first things that he does is asks to see the hands of those who had a good relationship with their father. I am told that though he has been doing this for a number of years since his retirement form the NFL, to date he has not had one single hand raised. This is an extremely serious correlation that vividly underscores the impact of fathers on their male progeny, especially in their absence.

However, though this book primarily focuses on male children we do not take lightly the impact of fathers on daughters. With that in mind it may serve the flow of ideas better if we first briefly address one of the most dramatic impacts of absent fathers on their female children. This will also dovetail neatly with our main focus because of the obvious and direct impact of young black females on young black males.

The absence of a father is clearly a problem that will affect female children in multiple areas. But I am convinced that one of the most significant ways it will be seen is in the way they choose mates. And it may be best illustrated in an observation of mine I call the *F.A.T* factor.

1. *The F.A.T. Factor:* Caring and present fathers usually provide daughters with the general framework or example for choosing the man that may become her future spouse. When fathers are never or rarely present, naturally mothers will most often provide daughters with their prime methodology for choosing a partner. I believe this is one of the core problems in this black

Foodservice worker phenomenon. To demonstrate this, we will look at a premise I have defined as the *Female Acceptance Threshold* or *F.A.T.* factor if you will. Simply stated, this is how much or how little the adolescent or adult female will accept pertaining to the adequacy standards of her male partner. Basically it is a measure of how little she is willing to settle for in a male.

From non-abusive fathers daughters tend to learn some of the basics of socializing with males and what to look for in a male partner. They usually learn how a man who respects them will treat them. They will also seek men who make them feel at least as secure as did their fathers. But in the absence of a father, females tend to learn most of what they know about or expect from men from their mothers or other prominent matriarchal figures in their lives. And if those icons have low *F.A.T.* factors, there is a strong likelihood that the female in question will also have a low *F.A.T.* factor as well. In other words, their toleration for the social and/or vocational inadequacies of male partners will allow for very low expectations to be placed on those partners.

We will discuss the *F.A.T.* factor more in depth when we investigate what non-abusive mothers bring to the basic family social unit.

This is important now however because this kind of thought process has the potential of producing generation after generation of young men with very little expectations beyond that of sex and/or sexual reproduction placed on them by females of their sub-culture or clique. Because in a subculture where the main indicators of achievement are ownership of designer logo clothing and the attaining of as many (high-risk) sexual encounters as possible, if these young men can have the esteem of comparable females without having any *realistic plans* for a viable future or extending any real commitment to her, then where is the motivation to healthily and legally improve his or her standard of living? **The less effort a male must put forth to attract the female (or females) of his choice, the less he will generally do.**

Realistic plans are plans that have some root in the present reality. For instance, if someone 16 or older tells you that they want to become a lawyer or a physician, where's the evidence of that today? Do they have grades that will get them into pre-law or premed? Are they taking college preparatory or prerequisite courses? Or do they just like watching Law and Order or ER on television?

2. ***Provider protector role:*** In the traditional family social unit the father is viewed in our society most often as being responsible for the overall wellbeing and safety of the family unit even if the mother works outside the home. And even though there are stay at home fathers, staying home is still an option largely afforded to women or mothers in families where the extra income is not needed to live at the economic level set or accepted by the family unit. Also, speaking of fathers as protectors, very few men would send their wives downstairs in the middle of the night to see what was moving around or making a noise. And most women would view a man who would do such a thing with disdain.

The average male is 1-3 times stronger than the average female. **(Research)** The dominant hormone in his body, testosterone, is dedicated to many things. One of them is the hardening of muscle tissue. He appears very early in life to be more aggressive than the average female. That he is a risk taker and a daredevil very early on may have something to do with the fact that on average he will run faster and jump higher than most of his female counterparts. So not only does society cast him in this role, his basic physiology also implies this. Some say that the male's strength and aggressive tendencies are holdovers from the times when we lived in caves and were hunter-gatherers. But if they are holdovers, what are they held over for? On the contrary I view the physical strength of males and the emotional intuitiveness of females as equal and opposite forces that bring balance and harmony. This kind of balance and harmony found in the traditional family setting wherein all our empirical data tells us that on average children grow and aspire better in.

Non-abusive fathers also teach their male children how to properly utilize their natural strength and comparative aggressiveness to the betterment of the family and society at large. Without this guidance they can and often do develop predatory tendencies and begin the practice of a type of natural selection (survival of the fittest) minus social constraints, i.e. extremely violent crimes. This is not a denunciation of Darwinist theory however. It is only an observation of facts in evidence in our society. For whether someone ascribes to Darwinism, Creationism, or Intelligent Design they wear their titles proudly and as Americans are all entitled to that freedom. There is one title however no one wants to wear however. And that is the title of *crime victim*. This is exactly what a "head in the sand" attitude about what is taking place around us can turn anyone into at any given time. We will discuss the matter of crime as it pertains to our topic more in depth in the chapter on Criminal Intent later in this book.

Of course some may think that the traditional **provider protector** role of fathers is antiquated. Especially in a time when many mothers not only work outside the home, but also have larger incomes than their spouses. I differ with this view regardless of how television, movies, and other entertainment forums seem to vigorously promote it. My reason for disagreement is simple and observable. Aside from the world of television and movies, I have noticed that in real life, and as stated earlier, sometimes you can easily have a family where

Jane Smith (wife) has an income that is greater than that of John Smith (husband). But if electricity is turned off in that home, more times than not the neighbors will say; "Look at what *Mr. Smith* allowed to happen to *his* family." Of course you can argue this point. But if you do, you will in my opinion, be in gross denial of the realities of our society.

3. ***Worth and imagery (the need to be noticed)*** – **A**ttempting to deny that fathers are usually the most dominant figures within the intact or closely connected family social unit is much like trying to deny that sports celebrities are role models. Deny it all you want but kids will still look up to and seek to emulate their favorite sports hero. Deny it all you want, but kids will still want a strong father who is protective, accessible, and who they can look up to, even if they never admit it to themselves or others.

Fathers can deny their impact on their children all they wish, it will not change the fact that what he thinks of them and communicates to them defines their sense of worth or lack thereof. In a family where the father ignores or puts down his children, mothers have to work tremendously hard to try and maintain or salvage the emotional stability of those children. But there are many times when, regardless of all the unconditional positive regard she may heap upon them, the damage can be pervasive and irreparable.

When fathers ascribe worth to their children they don't have to search for that sense of worthiness in other places, places like gangs, promiscuous relationships, and the temporary fantasy world of mood altering substances. The image of self that young people take from those environments always comes with dire, severe, and often lasting consequences.

But the human psyche will, being in many ways like water, seek its own level. We strive for level not necessarily functionality. By level I mean that we look for a place where the world around us actually makes sense. And though our "level" maybe viewed as dysfunctional by many, as long as it works for us is all that really matters. The problem shows up when we try and take our approach to life (that is borne from this skewed or dysfunctional perspective) out of our cliques and into the greater society. If those perspectives are dysfunctional enough in comparison with those of the greater society, we may find some tremendous and frustrating disappointments. For example, we may find that we are not afforded the rewards that come with good grades because studying is not a valued commodity within our clique or subculture. Or we are not rewarded with better jobs and promotions because preparation for such long-term goals is also not valued in the clique environment where immediate gratification is the norm.

Fathers' views are usually grounded in pragmatism. They tend to look at the world in less emotional terms. This pragmatism is often the basis of realistic goal setting. So, when this pragmatic view of life that is most often brought to the family social unit by the father is missing, it can and often does have the adverse affect of a lack of challenging or realistic goals set by their children. So even in the vacuum of *absentee fatherhood* we still see the profound effect of the role.

Also, absentee fathers tend to beget other absentee fathers. And so the low worth and imagery as manifested in a lack of *realistic goals* beget more would-be fathers with the same problems. They will often work in low paying jobs for most of their working lives, and more importantly, they will not be there for their children either.

- *Realistic goals are goals that are first and foremost achievable in the greater society without breaking the law or doing injury to others.*
- *Realistic goals are almost always definable by a series of smaller objectives or steps.*
- *And finally, they are goals that have no built in non-negotiable exclusions for the goal setter. For instance; someone setting a goal to become a police officer with a federal gun charge on his or her record.*

4. *The need to be noticed:* Music systems in the cars of youths have always been loud in comparison to those of older adults. This may be in part due to the additional stimulation required by the adolescent brain to not sink into boredom. It may also be a way of purposely annoying older adults for the sake of forcing them to take notice.

But why is it that the music systems in the cars of youths, especially African American youths are getting exponentially louder? Why is it that even on the hottest or coldest days many have their windows down to play these powerful systems to levels that call for everyone in their immediate vicinity and beyond to hear and notice them?

It is said by some that man has two basic psychological needs above all else. 1.) The need to love and 2.) The need to be loved by one other human being. If this is true, and I believe it is more true than untrue, what this says to me is that we all have a *need to be noticed.* Love in its' purest form after all is just paying more attention to the needs or wellbeing of another than your own. Love is making someone else feel special by ensuring that they are the true focus of attention. But what happens when an honest need goes haywire, consumes and colors all that a person or personality is because it is rarely if ever properly addressed?

In most intact or closely connected family social units, this attention normally comes from parents to children automatically and unconditionally. Children are loved. Their needs and wants are given the attention of their parents instinctively and involuntarily. It is not something that they normally have to work to obtain.

In the single parent household, responsible mothers are usually the only parents present. And many of them will also function toward their children in the same manner of extending unconditional love and attention. But here are the major problems that can and often do arise with this scenario. 1) It is obvious to both mother and child that the father is absent. 2) It is also obvious at both an instinctive and physical level that this should not be the case. 3) Mothers often either overcompensate for this, creating self-centered personalities in their children (which is only masking the need) or 4) they under compensate thereby making the child who is already bitter at some level for the lack of a father, even more bitter. This behavior is parental emotional apathy from both mother and father, and it is very dangerous.

In either case *the need to be noticed* and appreciated by their fathers become exasperated by bitterness or self-centeredness, both conditions demanding the fulfillment of the same need in their own way.

Why is it that the music systems in the cars of youths, especially African American youths, are getting exponentially louder? I believe it is nothing more than their attempt to address an honest need in one of the only ways they know and can control. The music is often filled with vulgar, inflammatory, and violent rhetoric. It is as if they are saying; *"Hey world! Look at me! I am important! I am bitter! I don't* *care! And I want you to know!* This is the message of someone that has been and is hurting.

We will address ***worth and imagery*** further in chapter two as it relates to a facet of human growth and development known as ***egocentrism*** under the section on ***Personality Disorders.***

5. **Reflective discipline** – Fathers are usually, but not always, the chief disciplinarian of a traditional family social unit since they do tend to bring more pragmatism to the overall child rearing experience. Non-abusive fathers are far more intent on using discipline as a tool to show their children what they can expect as a result of breaking the rules of society than to fuel his anger (Just the opposite of what is generally portrayed in entertainment media). His discipline reflects societal punishments for violating societal limits.

Why discipline? When someone violates a rule that has been established by self, the family unit, or society, guilt of conscience is usually one of the first emotional responses. The guilt can be uncomfortable at best and at worst, down right painful. It must and will be dealt with. You see the human psyche is similar in many ways to the human body. It also has significant self-healing properties. The problem in both instances however, is that the self-healing process is not always the best choice. Many times trained outside intervention is the better option. Hospitals would go out of business otherwise. For instance, when someone breaks a leg they can opt to splint it themselves and allow for the bone to knit itself back together. But there is a very good chance that the bone may knit back crookedly, not to mention the possibility of infection or irreparable tissue damage. For the sake of illustration, let us view the broken leg as an infraction of some type and the hospital intervention as the discipline necessary to address it properly.

Discipline helps alleviate the pain of guilt. It clears the conscience. It evens the score so to speak. The rule has still been broken, but the cost of the infraction has been paid, and all is right with the world. More importantly, the conscience of the individual often remains sensitive against committing that or similar infractions again. It is conditioned by the applied discipline and in all likelihood will seek to avoid the consequences of such behavior again.

But what happens when this healing of discipline is not applied? Well as I said, we will attempt to *self-heal.* That is, deal with the pain and/or discomfort of that guilty conscience in the most expedient way. One of the most expedient or common ways that the human psyche tends to deal with uncomfortable emotions or memories is through the psychological defense mechanism known as *suppression.* Simply explained, this is where the event or emotional response to the event is purposely and forcibly pushed below the level of conscience memory. The more common or recognized emotion this mechanism has been applied to is anger. In which event the more common terminology used to describe the process is called *"stuffing."* Stuffing the act of not processing the emotion in a healthy manner, but rather pushing it farther inwardly by playing down its importance often to the point where it is out of the realm on conscious thought… pretending it never happened.

Denial is another commonly utilized emotional defense mechanism. Basically, this is when we actually can see or recall the factual reality of past or present events but yet manage to convince ourselves either that it isn't happening or that the fallout is not as dire or extreme as others are making it out to be.

I have found that the basic practical difference between these two mechanisms is that *suppression* seems to manifest more as a sheer act of the will of an individual to forget an event, while denial often recognizes or recalls events but interprets them through "rose colored glasses." To accomplish this, individuals often have very definite statements that they make to themselves (self-talk) and convince themselves that these statements are true. For example; *"Looking back, I think that window was broken even before I threw that rock,"* or *"I'm positive it was Henry's rock that really broke that window. I'm sure his rock left his hand before mine did,"* or *"I would never have done anything like this if he hadn't made me so none of this is really my fault."*

The problem with suppression or denial of guilt is it hardens the conscience. Because the individual has purposely numbed himself to the pain of this infraction, he has virtually guaranteed himself, his family unit, and society that the next time he will be able to commit an even more serious offense. His conscience is conditioned, protected from responding with the same level of sensitivity as before to the same level of infraction. He has learned how to deal with the guilt of relatively lesser offenses. Now those offenses that may seem very serious to someone with a still sensitive conscience may appear to him minor in comparison.

How to discipline: As a parent and as a mental health professional that has worked extensively with the adolescent population. I find that very often when the term discipline is used in today's society it conjures up the act of corporal punishment. And corporal punishment has become the closet child of the disciplinary world. Very few parents will admit to using it because it is viewed by many as archaic, brutal, and not politically correct. I am not opposed to corporal punishment. It is not illegal and I believe that there is ample room to apply it safely and (by the way) lovingly. That being said, this section is not about corporal punishment but disciplining. Disciplining is a process. And as a professional and a parent I have also found that the type of disciplinary method utilized is very seldom where the process breaks down. Before the completion of this section I will prove this.

Disciplining can be best approached via a 7 Step process.

1. **Decide who administers** – The very first step in the disciplining process is to decide who will be responsible for administering it. There is of course the *"village concept"* which maybe fine if you live in a village. In that type setting there is probably a group or community consensus on the types of acceptable disciplinary methods, what punishments fit what infractions and clear boundaries about how far you may go in the process as an adult dealing with the child of one of your neighbors. But most of us don't live in a village and methods and boundaries can vary from household to household.

   In the event of single parents, mothers in particular, this responsibility will probably rest with her. But it can also be delegated to someone else such as a male relative she and her children respect, trust and who is involved on a regular basis with she and her children. In the event of married couples this is also something that should be discussed. Disciplining is tough work. Each partner may or may not share the same will to perform this necessary task of child rearing with equal resolve. The best case scenario is that among couples it is a shared and equal responsibility. But whichever option is chosen, here are a few simple rules to follow: **1.) If you are not the primary disciplinarian in your family social unit and an infraction occurs in that individual's absence, avoid terms such as, *"Just wait until your _____ gets home!* This can go a long way in our contemporary culture in making the other person out to be the heavy and demonstrate your lack of resolve to act authoritatively. Something your child will most certainly notice and may use in the future to play-up to you emotionally and attempt to split you adults concerning decisions in other matters. And if they are successful at this splitting, the process of disciplining will have been compromised and ineffective. The child will bring the adults to the point where they can't agree on anything, especially discipline. **2.) If you are not the primary disciplinarian still take *some immediate action in the interim* even if that simply sending the child to his or her room.** Failure to do *something* will make the adult present appear essentially powerless and not to be taken seriously. A statement such as; *"Go to your room. Your _____ and I will discuss this matter further when he (or she) gets home"* recognizes and preserves both the authority of the adult present and that of the prime authoritarian who is yet to arrive.

2. **Decide what works and doesn't work** – You may wish to seek assistance here from other parents who have children that adhere to and recognize their authority. They are obviously doing something that is yielding some positive results. There is also no harm in seeking the advice of qualified professionals that come with successful references from satisfied clients. Books on the topic that may be religious or secular in nature can also be good resources to utilize, especially when accompanied by the sound counsel and the guidance of someone else that has had real life practical applications and positive observable results using principles espoused in the work.

In working with adolescents and their families for a number of years, this was very often the step at which most parents said the process of disciplining their children broke down for them, and is reflected in statements like: "I've tried everything and nothing works!" or "I'm just at a loss as to what to try next… nothing works for this kid!" However, I can assure you that as important as methodology is it is not *the* most important step in the process. It is also not the place where the process most often breaks down, as I was able to show everyone of those exacerbated parents. We will shortly discuss where the does most often breakdown.

3. **Be timely** – Remember that one very important function of discipline is to alleviate guilt. And that if proper disciplining doesn't occur, our psyches will activate defense mechanisms to assist us with not feeling this emotional stress so we can function. So in our own way we have taken care of the problem. And now there can be a very real psychological disconnection from the event or infraction. Also, the lapse in time may allow the child to perform acts that he or she believes should have made up for the infraction. They may have caught up on chores, performed homework without any resistance, done non-solicited kindly acts for parents or siblings, etc. Now imagine the anger involved in someone disciplining you for a matter that by all accounts (at least in the mind of the child) has been taken care of. If discipline fails to be administered in a timely fashion, instead of correcting a child, a parent may only gain an enemy.

4. **Be consistent** – To illustrate this point please imagine a child in the grocery store line taking things repeatedly from the impulse buying shelves located near most cash registers. The mother however is repeatedly seizing the item(s) to restore to the shelf and all the while threatening punishment of some type (which she repeatedly fails to follow through with) if the child ever repeats the action - which of course he does. This ritual continues for a number of times until the mother finally and halfheartedly spanks

the hand of the child. Let us agree for the sake of argument that this ritual was repeated 9 times before the mother finally did what she stated she would do originally. Why shouldn't the child return to handling the impulse item(s) again? He probably will return to this behavior and he will do it for one reason only… a lack of consistency on the part of the mother. Yes, he was eventually punished. But he was punished only once for ten infractions, even though the parent promised punishment for all ten. Even a child can figure out that those are very good odds, and the odds are in his favor.

A lack of consistency is the main step at which the process of discipline most often breaks down. Yes. Make clear rules and set appropriate boundaries with proportionate consequences. But most importantly, be consistent in applying those consequences for the rules or boundaries that are violated.

"But what about *forgiveness?"* you may ask. Well, if by that you mean simply overlooking the infraction and foregoing the punishment I would advise against this. I do believe that sometimes foregoing the punishment may be appropriate, but overlooking the infraction is detrimental. If you think that your child deserves a break this time around because "everybody makes mistakes", this is fine when done sparingly. But the infraction should always be discussed. The child cannot have a true appreciation of the state of grace you just imparted to them if they have no respect for the rule or the boundary they broke. If you ignore discussing this (not badgering) they may ignore the value of the boundary.

6. **Avoid repeated use of your hands where possible** – Let me say again that I will not argue the pros and cons of corporal punishment in this book. However this step is

exclusively for those parents that find safely administered corporal punishment an acceptable form of discipline.

To begin with, it is very important in our extremely violent times for children to not perceive the bodies of their parent(s) as a source of pain, no matter how lovingly the punishment is applied. I am also not convinced that we possess the same temperament and restraints as did many of our fore-parents that allowed most of them to do this without violating the acceptable social limitations of their times. And obviously adult physiology and muscle structure, especially in males, is usually far more hardened and durable than are those of young children or adolescents. We're bigger and stronger and accidents can and do occur especially when there is such an obvious imbalance of power. But maybe just as important for fathers and mothers alike, the source of the disciplinary discomfort should be associated with something external to you. It is far easier to speak lovingly to your child before and/or after discipline has been administered to explain and discuss the matter (which is highly advised), if your child no longer has to view the instrument of his or her discomfort. This is a signal that the matter is settled and in the past. Nothing remains but a parent that loves them and only wants their wellbeing. And, who has also reluctantly gone through the process with them. However if your body is the direct source of that pain, the message can become very mixed and confusing. And your child could develop an unhealthy fear of your physical presence.

Let me restate. These are very different times. You cannot approach the use of physical force for any purpose the way it was approached even a generation ago. We interpret physical force differently today. Some of it is without a doubt political correctness. But much of it is because the level of violence against children in the form of physical abuse, abduction, molestation and murder at times appears to be spiraling out of control. Most children are deluged with the same news and information on this that parents are. And physical force for any purpose is likely seen as "evil" by many of the individuals that your child may come in contact with on a daily or regular basis. Of course physical force is neither evil nor good. It is neutral and depends solely on purpose and proportionality to define the ultimate nature of its use.

7. **Never discipline while angry-** I believe that there is such a thing as "righteous indignation" that is couched in altruistic or unselfish motives. Someone can be justifiably angry for the right reasons. In such circumstances, anger can become the inducement for them doing some very unselfish things. Many times however anger manifests itself as a very selfish emotion seeking only to satisfy the desire of the individual at the time. This type of anger is common to us all and much more likely to surface or occur than the more unselfish type of anger.

When we apply discipline in anger most likely it will be the selfish type. Our rules may have been broken, something of value to us may have been damaged, or our patience simply may have been stretched to the limit of its endurance. Our most potent desire at the time is to strike out at the apparent source of our problem in a vengeful manner with the sole aim of fixing things or evening up the score for our own sake, to make that individual pay for the discomfort they have caused us.

It is impossible to discipline in love and selfish anger simultaneously. Love has someone else as its focus. Selfish anger has only the punisher as its focus. The disciplinary process then becomes more about meeting our needs than the needs of someone else for guidance and correction.

In the case of parental disciplining, your motives will likely always be seen and felt by your child. They may be seen at the time you are administering the discipline or they may be seen in retrospect, but they will likely be seen. And again, if those motives reveal themselves as selfish and self-fulfilling versus loving and concerned, instead of correcting your child you will probably have made an enemy or at the least created someone that views you as more of a bully than a parent.

A simultaneous equation: In the history of our nation, except during the brief era known as *Reconstruction,* blacks have never been represented in the professional and political ranks more than they are today. At the same time, the sociological concept of *"Future Shock"* applied to the national vocational landscape of the not so distant future is worth noting and extrapolating upon here, for the advancing devastating or negation of this progress is happening not under the radar, but right in front of us. Follow me on this. The increase of single parent African-American households is happening at a much faster rate than are traditional households. And all this is happening far more rapidly than society can adjust to, as evidenced in one facet by our overburdened criminal justice system that has a disproportionately high African-American population, which cannot be solely attributed to racial prejudice. So if single parent households where these lower echelon food service workers mostly come from are on the increase at a higher rate than traditional households, then what is the vocational landscape for blacks going to look like one, two, or three decades down the road? As the households that on average produce the lawyers, physicians, engineers, and other professionals continue to simultaneously shrink in comparison to those households that produce the long-term foodservice workers, what is the logical conclusion here? And are we satisfied with this imminent and mind staggering outcome? Where have all the fathers gone?

My Father's Funereal

I remember being seated next to my mother
her squeezing my hand until it hurts
as they lowered him slowly

Her other hand lay atop a folded flag on her lap
that all before had been draped across his box
That cold box

I remember tears falling from beneath a black vale
and a young woman sniffling to remain strong
In the face of her loss

I remember music about sweet by and byes
And my brother's short black pants
My sister's bewildered look

I remember black.
And my father sinking slowly
from out of our sight.

E. Middleton

What non-abusive mothers bring to the unit

When we acknowledge that nearly 70% of all children being born to black females in America are being born into single parent households where mothers or grandmothers are heads of household, it becomes extremely important and on balance to take a close look at the pieces that the non-abusive mother brings to the family social unit.

1. ***Primary caregivers:*** In our formative years, from infancy through early childhood, mothers are the primary care givers for most of us. And since the mother and child union has been physiologically established since conception and

psychologically established at some point during the gestational period, it appears a logical, natural, and mostly seamless carryover for both of them postpartum.

But it is more than that. The female brain seems uniquely wired for this task. It is at least wired differently from those of males, with many believing that difference is precisely why women make better primary caregivers to children in their formative years. Males tend to have less cross talk between the right and left brain which can produce a linear approach to problem solving (i.e. a tendency of never going to B before A is completed). It's almost like the difference between baseball and soccer with male mentality being that of a baseball diamond and female mentality being the soccer field. There is a home plate in baseball that the runner must cross to score but to do so he must touch first, second, and third bases in that order. On the soccer field there is also a goal that you must put the ball into in order to score, and generally you must head in that direction. But on the way, there are many, many routs down the course and many, many directions the ball can turn before the kicker ultimately scores. Both ways make perfect sense to both athletes and ultimately produce the same results. They just arrive at it differently. And please keep in mind that these are generalities. I am not trying to typecast everyone in a specific gender or a specific sport.

Males also tend to use words and express emotions less than females. Primary caregivers of very young children have to be in tune and aware of the ambient environment as well as the child. They may be required to talk on the phone, while preparing a meal, and still be expected to respond emotionally to a child who just skinned their knee.

During this formative time, children learn and systematize information stemming from a growing awareness of self and their environment. They also learn how to relate to that environment. Mothers model behavior and assist our brain in making sense of the world around us. We also learn early on from her about other concepts such as setting, observing, and maintaining appropriate *boundaries.* We learn about *sharing.* And even the act of learning itself can be both encouraged and reinforced by her or conversely, treated as something that has little to no priority.

2. *A sense of steadfastness:* While fathers bring a sense of *security* mother bring a sense of *steadfastness* which is mainly developed through the child watching her day after day performing the tasks that provide comfort and wellbeing to the family unit. It is also the knowing of the child of her availability and emotional connection to the moment of their discomfort or suffering that promotes calm and reassured young minds.

    Working mothers may not have the immediacy to their children as stay at home mothers do, but they often are the ones that make the trips to and from the daycare, school, or pediatrician. And it is that expectation from her children that she will always arrive at or near a certain time each day with an almost immediate emotional connection regardless of what her own day has been like and this creates almost the same sense of steadfastness and reassurance. This doesn't negate the need for the *Provider/Protector* roles of fathers, but compliments it.

3. *Dual roles:* When the father is absent the mother must now provide both of these roles. The problem with this scenario is that female children will often emulate their mothers and learn the two roles providing both overall security and steadfastness. Male children in this same absentee father scenario, and with no responsible male role model, will often learn neither. Especially if he is in a subculture where his closest male friends come from the same type of family social units. Those young males will often seek to emulate prominent male figures

valued by their subcultures. Most of them will likely be from the sports and/or entertainment world. For these are the largest pools of images of older males they will most consistently be exposed to. These icons will also all too often become their definitions of success. Not only do some of these same icons promote lifestyles and philosophies that perpetuate out of wedlock births, they are also from industries with extremely high failure rates. Most children who play sports or music will never sign a professional contract or make a living wage in either industry. And while no child should be discouraged from pursuing honest vocational goals, whenever possible they should do so with the pros and cons fully and realistically explained to them by responsible adults with a legitimate interest in their future.

Females learning both roles now become the dominant figures in the family structure. Males are then released from their natural roles of providers of overall security or the *Provider/Protector* role. This is at best a dysfunctional arrangement and absent of balance. Daughters are taught that their need for males can be reduced to the basics of sexual attraction, sexual gratification, and reproduction (if the pregnancy is not aborted). This is also one of the primary mindsets that allow sons to live out the animal or "dog" role glamorized into today's pop culture music. He is freed to only seek and bring sex to a relationship rather than the love, caring, and security necessary for a balanced, functional family.

This characterization promotes the concept of boys and young men as only animals in their approach to life and the opposite sex, specifically "dogs." The broad acceptance of this concept is also what I believe makes it easier and easier for popular music artist to refer to women repeatedly and unashamedly in their music as "bitches" (female dogs). And if the young males in question are only animals then why shouldn't they behave as such? They have a built in excuse. It is not only what they have been taught, but in many cases the only expectation that has been placed on them by their subculture, specifically the females in them. Be true to your culture. In a very real sense it is what we are all taught. Be "true" to your crowd - one of the primary rules of indoctrination. And with the young men we are discussing, all too often living up to any other better expectation is interpreted as "trying to be white."

4. ***Choosing a mate - The Female Acceptance Threshold (The F.A.T. Factor):*** I have observed that in choosing a male partner many young African American females' expectations seem either so low comparatively speaking or so unrealistic that they are virtually assured of a negative outcome. By negative outcome I mean forming a relationship with a male that will happily utilize them for sex, convenience, and possibly even financial support while keeping them in an atmosphere of economic insecurity and devoid of achievable short or long- term goals. Goals as simple and normal as saving for retirement, college for their children, home ownership, dream vacations etc. will likely fail to materialize for them. And if they do actualize them, more than likely they will have to be the primary provider of them.

It appears they tend to choose male partners more on physical appearance, physical prowess, and smooth talk rather than on identifying males with honest and realistic goals who are visibly forging legal opportunities for their futures.

As explained earlier the ***Female Acceptance Threshold or F.A.T. factor,*** is the level of inadequacy that the female is willing to accept in current or potential male partners. So prior to going further we should seek to briefly define inadequacy. Webster defines the term as, "Not adequate" or "insufficient." For the sake of our discussion I believe that it can be characterized by some or all the following: *The clear inability or unwillingness of the male to discipline himself sexually,* *emotionally, spiritually or educationally and provide financial security for his female partner and children in a marital relationship involving license and legal ceremony.*

You must remember that in the type family social unit we are examining in this book, just having the male there in the household on a part time basis is looked upon as a major plus for him and for the family unit. His total absence and/or non-involvement takes him no lower than par with her (his child's mother) as well as with his extended social circles of friends and other family members. This is undoubtedly an unforeseen ripple effect of the former welfare state when welfare recipient mothers were rewarded for having no permanent adult male figures in their domiciles and penalized for the converse. For generations it was to a mother's advantage, at least financially, not to have the father (or fathers) of her children as constant figures within the home. She was also rewarded more financially each time she repeated the ritual of having a child with no marital ties to the father and no visible means of support for that child.

So, part time and absentee fatherhood which by their very nomenclature and design are **substandard has become the new standard** in a large segment of African American culture. This by the way is the same segment of society that will ultimately produce most of the young men that will fill prisons and Fast Food employee roles for inordinately long periods of time now and in the future unless change takes place.

Women with low *FAT factors* tend to more readily accept men into their lives as long term partners with some or all of these characteristics:
- No pledge of marriage anywhere on the horizon,
- No steady and substantial means of support,
- No transportation,

- Very little education,
- Active substance abuse disorders,
- Violent and abusive temperaments and more.
- Misguided Priorities such as: *a cell phone with no transportation, spending more on wants than needs, finds it hard to distinguish between needs and wants, believes that sex is far more important than marriage etc.*

Accordingly, males presenting with many or all of these characteristics will also be prime candidates for lower echelon foodservice jobs and will also be prime candidates for biologically reproducing more low echelon foodservice workers.

The best case scenario appears to be that young females should be educated on how to choose male partners that will have realistic prospects of legally achieving lifestyles that will allow for the proper care and support of a family in a marriage relationship. Remember, statistically speaking, children from this kind of environment tend to perform much better in life than do their contemporaries coming from single parent households. Those are the facts. And they are undisputed.

Marriage and divorce

The newest Census Bureau statistics say that for the first time more women (51%) are living without husbands. This doesn't mean that 51% of all women aren't married. The numbers include for instance women whose husbands are incarcerated, deployed militarily, and women who are separated but not divorced. The actual number of unmarried women more realistically could be 35-40%. This is still a significant number. Such factors are sited such as: women marrying later for the sake of careers, more women cohabiting, the ease of no-fault divorces, divorced women remarrying less than others. They also state that only 30% of

African-American females are married and that number is far below Asian, Hispanic, and Caucasian women. The Bureau sites trends such as the rising number of African-American males being incarcerated while more African-American females are receiving a college education only to find themselves with no comparable partners. I think that they are ignoring some other obvious reasons for this trend nationally and among African-American demographics.

1. ***Males do most of the asking*** – It is a cultural norm and expectancy in western civilization that males do the majority by far of proposing marriage. Although I have heard of instances where females have "popped the question" I am certain this is the exception and not the rule. One obvious cause of fewer marriages that no one appears to be mentioning is that *fewer men are asking*. But why is this? I believe some of the reasons are:

   - Men are finding it easier to move from relationship to relationship because there are more available women than there are men and most of them appear to be willing to cohabit without marriage.
   - Many men find live-in relationships more to their advantage because they are most times far less liable financially if and when the relationship fails.
   - Many men are a contradiction and largely hypocritical when it comes to multiple relationships. But due to popular culture's acceptance of pre-marital sex (supposedly for both sexes) individuals are now likely to participate in several sexual relationships prior to marriage. Most men while approving this behavior in themselves and other males do not necessarily see it as a plus in the woman that they desire to marry no matter what they may outwardly verbalize in order not to appear archaic or Victorian in their world views.

2. ***Faith prohibitions:*** Religious as well as secular society appears affected by these numbers. Marriage and divorce within local congregations currently seem to closely mirror the trends reflected in society at large. But because there are often significant differences in the moral or relational codes of both groups it stands to reason that some of the causes of divorce maybe different also and that is the focus of this section.

For the sake of discussion, since churches significantly outnumber synagogues and mosques in this country, I will be utilizing them as my primary point of focus in this part.

First I want to acknowledge that I have found the church to be one of the most compassionate and loving places in society. Most congregations I know would do their level best to meet an individual or community need of which they have been made aware. And the points I will discuss in this segment in nowise should be seen as anything more than what it is in every other segment of this book: the address of forces impacting the formation of families so that we all might be the beneficiaries of positive change wherever it might be warranted.

Many men and women with deep spiritual convictions have definite religious constraints on who they can and cannot marry and are choosing to act on those convictions. Usually they are not only required by doctrine to marry someone of the same faith but must also be sure on a spiritual level that this is the individual God has chosen for them. Yet the availability of acceptable mates appears to be declining in the faith community also. Some reasons may be:

- ***Attendance and participation in local congregations are down*** nationally for most of organized religion. And in most congregations women tend to be the majority of those who are attending. Of the men who are attending most of them tend to be already married or at least in serious relationships that have the promise or potential of marriage. I believe that religious assemblies are still a good place to locate a mate yet all the while noting that this should not be the prime reason for affiliation. If finding a mate is the primary reason for an individual's religious affiliation and attendance, this can be obvious. Such individuals may present as not being comfortable with their singleness, can often appear desperate or odd, and tend to scare off potential mates.

But there is also the *"Pop Culture"* fantasy ideal mate image that churchgoers are not immune to. Some invariably hang on and wait for this image while talking themselves and others into believing the notion that they are indeed "waiting on God."

I am convinced that one of the main things that led to and preserved marriage in the past for our culture were the complimentary perspectives shared by single males and females of the time. With earlier generations, in general, men when seeking a mate tended to be looking for someone to love. And conversely women tended to be looking for someone to love them. That has changed. Now women (and there are many reasons for this) seem to have the same perspective as men when seeking a mate and in other areas. But when men view women as coming from the same perspective as them relationally, one that has been conventionally masculine, they may be far less apt to feel needed in the role of *provider protector*. This is not to say that single congregational women need to walk around with their heads bowed in the presence of eligible males projecting an image of neediness. But what it is saying is that there is a need sometimes for a different perspective. In this case the perspective of older women within their congregations maybe helpful and able to add some balance to their own. With changed perspective, changed affect and behavior usually follow naturally.

But this type of older generation exposure and subsequent learning from is becoming more and more difficult for younger females as well as males in congregations to access. Most congregations I am aware of that have 200 or more in regular attendance seem so segmented by age groups that the only significant exposure and exchange one has to the other is at special events. One older parishioner that I have regular conversations with, when speaking of her Sunday school class, has often said, *"They just stick us away in our own little cubby holes and nobody really wants to come near us. They all are afraid. I think we remind them too much of what it is to grow old."* So in the part of the religious or worship experience that is most designed for the learning experience, the advantage that is gained through those with more life experience is exchanged for the comfortableness found in sameness.

Also the word "love" has taken a predominantly emotional meaning, the problem with this being that emotions tend to wax hot and cold. There was a time, however, when a large portion of relational love involved the *will* or cognitive portion of the psyche. Individuals decided to perform acts and behave in a manner indicative of love even when the emotional connection was not there at the time. When love is relegated to an emotion only, this kind of behavior can be seen as rote or even hypocritical. When love is perceived as a part of the will, the same behavior can be seen in the more noble and altruistic lights of duty and commitment. This is a lost and quickly dying art in contemporary marital unions. We seem to have almost forgotten the ability to think and act altruistically in our relationships. It's certain if we don't know behavior, it cannot be modeled or passed on to others.

- ***The unpardonable sin approach to divorce may also be a factor.*** Many well-meaning churches can take a rather harsh and/or non-scriptural approach to this often-devastating event that can alienate the divorced parishioner. This harshness can demonstrate either a lack of knowledge or an unwillingness to receive the true teachings of scripture on this topic, albeit with the often honorable motive and intent of discouraging divorce. I think for many who are married it does just that. But for the divorced individual it often creates unwarranted stigmas, discouragement, and a real fear of ever taking a spouse again, something that is never prohibited to Christians when they've divorced according to scriptural allowances for the same. There is a great possibility that some regular attendees who have chosen to either cohabit or maintain low profile intimate relationships outside of marriage have taken note of this. They see how they may also be perceived and what would be their own treatment within the congregation if they themselves are ever the survivors of an unfortunately failed marriage. Speaking with these couples is often difficult because most of the time it's the female partner who attends services alone. But when I had the occasion to speak with them together they usually make statement like, *"We know it's wrong but marriage is a big step, we just don't want to wind up divorced."*

The stigma attached to divorce manifests itself in many denominations by basically limiting divorced parishioners in the level of responsibility that they are able to ascend to or maintain. To exact this penalty denominations often focus on scriptures that list qualification for church leadership such as 1 Timothy 3:2 and Titus 1:6 (KJV) *"...the husband of one wife..."* a scripture that must be removed from the context in which it was written to arrive only at that interpretation. In context, Paul the Apostle to the Gentiles (all who are not Jews or Samaritans), wrote this scripture into a culture where the Romans, who were monogamous, ruled over cultures who were polygamous. Germans, Hebrews and others allowed for multiple wives and the concubine system. And it is extremely possible that this is what the Apostle was referring to. This would also be logical from the standpoint of how much time must be given to produce and maintain just one healthy functional family. If a man had several families to contend with he would obviously be a poor choice for leadership because he would probably neither lead well at home or in the local congregation, as time would be a premium and against him in both positions.

The popular traditional view of this scripture is "... that a pastor must not be divorced and remarried... If he cannot rule his own house how can he rule the church (Liberty Bible Commentary 1982, p644)?" Yet I have seen pastors that have become divorced, through no fault of their own, which have never remarried and continued to lead their congregations only to be criticized by those claiming the love and grace associated Christianity. Ultimately spouses are individuals who will make up their minds for themselves if they want to continue in a fidelity-based relationship or not. Just because someone has the spiritual gift of pastor and watches over their respective households well it doesn't mean that they can force someone else to remain with them or their family. In the Christian faith the Pastor is symbolic of Christ as the head of the church. Yet no one foolishly seeks to remove Him (Christ) from His exalted Headship because in much of Christendom the church as a whole as well as its' individual members continually, each in their own time, "plays the harlot" and forsakes Him and his commandments.

In this approach to divorce, remarriage is also either forbidden or frowned upon. So the stigma is only heightened for divorced congregational members because some pastors view a ceremony involving someone that has been previously divorced as somewhat messy or burdensome in terms of having to determine the circumstances under which the divorce took place and may just opt out of performing the ceremony altogether. (Notwithstanding that it is arguably a given that it is a pastor's duty to investigate the problems and needs of members.)

But the more notable point is that all this is done in spite of the fact that sacred Christian scriptures allow for divorce under two circumstances: adultery Mt. 19:9 (KJV) *"...Whosoever shall put away his wife, except it be for fornication, and shall marry another commiteth adultery..."* and abandonment 1 Cor. 7:15 (KJV) *"But if the unbelieving depart, let him depart. A brother or sister is not under bondage in such cases."* And in at least one instance clearly states that remarriage is not a sin 1 Cor. 7:27-28 (KJV) 27) *"Art thou bound to a wife? Seek not to be loosed. Art thou loosed from a wife? Seek not a wife.* 28) *But and if thou marry, thou hast not sinned:"* Notice that "bound" refers to marriage and "loosed" to divorce (Liberty Bible Commentary 1982, p434).

The looming paradoxical question that overshadows all of this may be summed up as such. It is doubtful whether the God of Sacred Christian Scriptures would provide instructions on how to sin or transgress against Himself. So since divorce and remarriage if done according to Sacred Text could not be a transgression or sin, why are some penalized and/or ostracized for it? What is the basis for supporting this behavior?

Marriage is surely one of the greatest institutions afforded to humanity and worthy of the struggle that it often times takes to preserve it and its' sacredness. But if my limited understanding of scriptures is correct it is not greater than God or the concept of Grace. The *unpardonable sin approach* can harm many divorced individuals that could be of great use in local congregations across the spectrum of spiritual gifts and responsibilities and in new relationships that could yield healthy functional families.

It would seem that one way to avoid this approach is to avoid distorting the spiritual hierarchy that in descending order of awareness proceeds God, marriage (and other God breathed institutions), sin, and Grace into a construct where marriage becomes the god, divorce the unpardonable sin, and Grace becomes non-existent. In sacred text when Jesus was looking for someone to evangelize in the Samaritan town of Sychar, he did not go to the upstanding citizens of that place, He went to a woman who had five divorces and at least one incident of cohabitation in her background (John 4:1-29) who had believed and received His message.

And I am aware that many good hearted people have what they believe to be very good reasons for taking this approach to divorce and they certainly don't identify it with the same phrase that I have utilized, or consciously mean it within themselves. But it is my belief and personal experience that in the end the

treatment of divorced individuals, in general, implies this phrase for the reasons I have attempted to cover here and do so without malice.

CHAPTER II
Psychological Aspects

Environmental Reinforcements

Some researchers believe that our brain is just one huge association making apparatus. That is, it tries to make sense of the world around us, our ambient environment, based on relating one element to another largely through sensory inputs and memory in ways that explains it. For instance, if you walked into a room and there was only money and a table, and having never seen either before your brain through your eyes would start receiving sensory information and also begin trying to define their forms and relationships to each other in a way that worked for you. It would try to accomplish this in a way that would help you in reaching your psychological level if you will, much in the way that water seeks its' own level. To others you may later encounter your use cr uses for these two things, the money and the table, may seem ludicrous, but based on the information that you had at the time when you first encountered these items it is perfectly rational, at least to you. You may rationalize for instance that the table is something to sleep on and the money (in large enough amounts) is something either to rest your head on or to cover yourself with. And if this rationalization of use(s) continues to "work" for you and has been positively reinforced over time it can become a behavioral pattern that is difficult to eradicate or even alter to any noticeable degree.

We are all impacted to one degree or another by most of the elements of our environment. We try to make sense of it all. What these environmental elements mean to us as well as those around us is a question that parents help our brains to work out with proper resolution. They provide information and insight that will assist us in making socially acceptable associations and coming to positive and edifying conclusions. Through them we can see the world as most people around us see it. Because of this we can make healthy decisions, set realistic goals, and claim the honest rewards of our society.

However when that parental support and direction is not there these environmental factors don't go away. In fact, it is my opinion that in this void they often make a larger and far more problematic impact. These associations are then usually solved for young people today by the entertainment media and/or others in their subculture or clique.

This section will seek to examine the impact of some of the more prominent environmental factors facing the impressionable adolescents and young adults who reside in the void created by a lack of balanced parenting. The first three of these factors are considered to be reinforcements because there are actual rewards associated with them within the contemporary social sub-culture that means most to the individual. These rewards seem to far outweigh the consequences to the young people buying into them. The sub-culture's acceptance strengthens their self-image, pathological though it may be. So this dysfunctional behavior of the individual is encouraged, and in a kind of closed loop not only validates but also shapes their worldview. Because at the end of all of this is the matter of acceptance, something that is always very high on the list of rewards for we humans.

1. **Peer association** – It is perfectly normal for adolescents to rebel against the status quo of the family social unit and society. It is one of the ways that we struggle for independence and individuality. In many cases during this stage of human development we may test and reject many values that have been taught to us since birth. We often signal our disconnection with our *old values* and the family social unit in displays of different and often extreme clothing, music, speech etc. Most of the time the place where we obtain our *new values* is from our contemporary peer group, who, for the population we are discussing appears more and more to be getting these values from media entertainment, which is a for profit industry. That

is an important fact and one that will be discussed more in the next section on music.

But for most of us this rebellious period is only a phase. By the time we are well into adulthood we have come back to the basic values of our family social units. This is why so many of us are stunned to find out at a certain age that we have actually become our parents! Fewer places is this more evident than the times we speak to our own children and hear the very words come out of our own mouths that were spoken to us by our parents only one short generation before... scary.

But when we return from our adolescent/young adulthood experimentation with values, we often will bring back ideas and values with us that were never our parents. These are the things that make us unique individuals. However it should be noted that we could bring back both positive and/or negative values. And both the positive and negative can stay around forever. For instance, sometimes an individual can bring back an addiction into a family system where work ethic is prized above almost everything else. And what you could wind up with is a functional addict. This can be defined or manifested as someone who gets up and goes to work each day but comes home and by night terrorizes their spouse and children with their own intoxicated behavior.

This is why peer group association in the adolescent period is so very important. While it would be a mistake in most cases (not all) for parents to choose their children's friends, conversely it would be negligent and risky not to establish some basic ground rules when it comes to socialization outside of the home. Some basic checkpoints such as meeting your children's friends face to face, knowing their addresses, phone numbers, parents, and maintaining realistic curfews are just a few safeguards.

Parents should always be able to present their children with clear and concrete reasons for an objection to a peer they would rather them not associate with. *"Because I said so"* is not always the first best option. I do recognize however that at times there may be friends, or prospective friends, whose behaviors are so dangerous, promiscuous, or unlawful that parents would be justified in taking immediate steps to prohibit their children's association with them. But most times this is not the case for children in traditional family units. So, absent these elements in their *unsavory* friend's behavior, parents may wish to assume the role of advisor on what to expect in the way of consequences for maintaining such peer associations. We should also make sure that through our attitudes we leave the lines of communications open as to always provide our children with a way back home. This way if and when by their own experiences they make the similar assessments as we did, not only can they abandon the relationship without looking foolish or weak, but can also return and discuss some of their disenchantment and learning with us without running smack dab into an *"I told you so."*

Keep in mind that this book examines some of the impacts of the unbalanced family where the father is absent. So what we are talking about often, not always, is a family with a high degree of innate dysfunction. Now what happens when both the family and peer group is unbalanced and seriously dysfunctional?

Well, to help us navigate this with more clarity and ease, let me introduce one of the tools I really like in the mental health diagnostic process. It is called the *GAF (Global Assessment of Functioning)*. This is basically a measure of how well we do individually with day to day personal and societal living or how impaired or dysfunctional we are. It asserts that all of us are on a continuum (a line with a sliding scale in either direction) when it comes to being functional or dysfunctional.

It is a considered a continuum because everyone everywhere is always on it. This continuum's scale ranges from 0-100. A score of 100 is representative of Mr. or Ms. Perfect with no symptoms of impairment, and 0 represents someone who is at or near room temperature. On a good day most of us pan out somewhere between the mid 70's and high 80's.

You don't see real SERIOUS symptoms or impairments until you reach 50 heading south. This is where you may have serious problems in any one or a combination of the following areas: social, occupational, or educational. You don't interact well with others, or you can't keep a job, or you have done very poorly with regard to your education.

Serious problems in any one or a combination of these areas can present really tough barriers to living a healthy and rewarding lifestyle. It can block the establishment and pursuit of goals that do not conflict with the law or the rights of others. And it only sets the stage for further decline on the continuum.

In the 40s we begin to see MAJOR impairment in several areas such as employment or education, family relations, judgment or mood. As an adult this individual can have periods of depressed moods, neglects their family, and is unable to work. As an adolescent they frequently beat up younger kids (bullying), are defiant to parents, and probably failing at school.

Generally speaking most mental health professional will utilize the *CGAS (Children's Global Assessment Scale)* to assess functioning in children under the age of 18. This scale is consistent with the *GAF* in that it also sites *major impairment* as behavior consistent with scores below 40. However, the functioning elements get far more age relevant. It states: *40-31 Major impairment of functioning in several areas and unable to function in one of these areas (i.e., disturbed at home, at school, with peers, or in society at large, e.g., persistent aggression without clear instigation; markedly withdrawn and isolated behavior due to either mood or thought disturbance, suicidal attempts with clear lethal intent; such children are likely to require special schooling and/or hospitalization or withdrawal from school (but this is not a sufficient criterion for inclusion in this category).*

Let's make the supposition that a household is much like a person in that it also has a level or degree of functioning. Now if the household function at or near 50 and an adolescent within the household has a peer group which functions in the *40s* what is the logical outcome? Minus some kind of external intervention, where on the continuum will this individual function for the majority of his adolescence and young adulthood phases of life? And when he matures to full adulthood what will be his options?

2. **Music *(and the need to be noticed)*** – Second only to peers, is the next strong and pervasive environmental reinforcement affecting this group… music. It is reinforcement and not merely entertainment for many young people because instead of taking on the form of entertainment it very often instructs and validates them.

The art form of music has always provided the youth of most civilized or industrialized cultures with a method to state the views of their generation. There is nothing unusual about this. But with the advent of the information age and 3rd generation electronics (IC Chips) music is available on demand not only via radio and stereo, but through MP3 players, satellite, computers, TV, the Internet and cellular phones. Its' constancy and ready availability allows it to speak to and instruct more children in the course of a day than do many parents.

Musical entertainment is a thriving for-profit industry. As a capitalist I find nothing wrong with the notion of building a better mousetrap or the profit motive associated with it. However in my opinion there is a point where responsibility ought to override the self-satisfaction and gratification of profit. And even though we are currently discussing the music entertainment industry, there are also other industries that seem to be *missing the sense of responsibility that is driven by conscience.* When profit margin or ideological agenda is the only thing that drives a business, then it can create serious problems for the society from which it draws its' customer base, though it may succeed in offsetting at least the accountability for these problems it willingly creates with obligatory gestures in the form of comparatively small charitable donations or funding community based projects, most of which are tax deductible. For instance, people can become addicted to many things. But when the chief tool for customer return sales is a continued addiction to the product being sold, *I believe that particular business or industry is operating without conscience.*

I don't want to get into the specifics of naming companies or organizations here. There is a place for that but not in this work. This book is about concepts, ideas, and ideology that we have allowed to become accepted and pervasive, and that are causing us harm as a society. It is about our very approach to life as a culture and some of the changes we must make to ensure our survival. For if a chain is truly only as strong as its weakest link, a people are only as strong as the weakest among them.

Making changes will take time. But if we get bogged down in doing war with a specific company or organization without first openly owning the problem in whatever venue or public forum that makes itself available to us, we pass the blame, remaining in denial. And don't be discouraged at the size of your audience. It may be an audience of one or one million. But social change is about an idea that captures the hearts and souls of a people, one individual at a time.

The focus of this section is mostly on the music entertainment industry only because it is such a major part of the lifestyle of the adolescent and young adult males at the heart of this discussion. All that having been said, we can now move forward into our discussion.

Music has become much louder and much more vulgar today. But no one barring a recipient of the profits of popular music (including and especially rap/hip-hop) or a fan, can say with any degree of honesty that this increase in volume and vulgarity has been a simple linear and normal progression from the last generation until now. Generations, depending on the source you use will cover anywhere from 16-40 years. When I was a teenager in the late sixties through the mid-seventies most songs were about emotional love. Now most songs that I hear that age group listening to are about sex, materialism, and violence; in that order. And what *has* happened to bring this about in my estimation is just as important what *is* happening because of it.

In chapter one under the section about *"Non-abusive Fathers"* we looked at how music, in the absence of a good father, can be used by the young consumers we are addressing as a way of meeting a natural and functional need in a rather dysfunctional manner. So I will now attempt to explain what I believe to be the basis for this digression from the music production end of the equation. And also hopefully show how it is a principal factor in many of the negative outcomes we are currently witnessing specific to young African America males from single parent households. There is a *need to be noticed*.

Some industries appear to operate on the principle of stimulating base negative sensations and emotions in their consumers. They may focus on emotions such as fear, anger, hatred or unfettered sexual desires. The problem is that whenever you make your business predominately one of sensual stimulation **you must continually "up the anti" so to speak.** The reason for this is that exposure to a stimulus often will cause us to become slightly desensitized to it with each exposure. So, to produce the same reaction as before we must be exposed to a stronger stimulus than the previous. This **tolerance** is highly observable in substance abuse and other forms of addiction. And if some portions of the music entertainment industry were headed in this direction before the advent of rap and hip-hop, the speed at which it was moving increased exponentially with the ascension of this art form and lifestyle. This falls into an information cluster I have identified as *Shock Media Entertainment*. Some others in this grouping would be; the newer more violent reality police shows, scare tactics TV, relational infidelity shows, daytime live audience talk shows, and also some major news media outlets.

I identify these enterprises as *Shock Media Entertainment* because **they are the segments of the information and entertainment industry that earn their profits by shocking the senses**. Often they purport to only be reflecting life. This is only partially true. Most of the things that they report, sing, or talk about don't happen to the majority of the populace, but usually only a small segment of it. The portion of the society that is going about life in some pretty usual and positive ways is focused on much less than are the negative aspects of society. However, those companies/organizations that does earn their living by keeping their customers whipped into frenzy or believing that they are the focus of some vast nefarious conspiracy, also convince those same customers that they are the only ones with the facts and therefore are indispensable.

In the case of the mainstream press, I avoid listening, watching, or reading it as often as possible. One of the main reasons for this is that it depresses me. For a long time I was confused and troubled by this until I analyzed the situation. I came to the conclusion that for the most part the news is about death and crime, in other words the obituaries and the police blotter. Well, I already knew that people were dying. And I already knew that people were being locked up. And even in the event that this was happening to someone close to me I had never found this information out in the media, but had always gotten it post haste via friends and family members. So why did I need the almost constant drumbeat of all this negativity pounded into my consciousness multiple times daily?

Lest I be remiss, not all media news is negative. Based on this truth I limit, not eliminate my exposure to the news. And I feel better because of it.

Specifically in reference to rap music and hip-hop culture, most people outside that culture don't carry weapons, want to kill policemen, use profanity on a regular basis, speak about women in extremely derogatory terms, wear gaudy ornate jewelry and the list goes on. And I don't think that all the aforementioned apply to all rap artists or hip-hopper. But it is what is heard in much of the lyrics. It is also the public image of many of its icons.

As alluded to earlier, I know that every generation has its own musical signature. This is nothing new. However what we are talking about is not the natural generation gap of music but the continuous exposure of a vulnerable portion of the population to lyrics that to them become actual instructions because they do not have the backdrop of a balanced family from which to gain true perspective. The lyrics become the reality because often there is no place to look in the immediate environment that shows them that most people who truly want something honest and positive out of life don't think or behave this way.

3. ***Self defacement (The need to be noticed):*** The term *defacement* is used here in the clinical sense denoting the cutting, tearing, penetrating, severing, or marring of the skin or body in any way that is possibly connected to or caused by neurosis. That being said, tattooing and piercing is nothing new to humanity. Permanent cutting or etchings into the skin as well as making holes in the skin to place jewelry or other objects of adornment into can be seen in many primitive as well as advanced cultures. In our culture this practice is obviously rabidly increasing. Since by all accounts our society is becoming increasingly neurotic it is reasonable to assume that some of this behavior is also increasingly neurotic in nature. So many individuals have left the realm of using these practices for adornment and aesthetics to using them as a major way of expressing messages of self-perception and deeper problems of the psyche. In many ways it is like the person who constantly uses profanity in their speech. He or she is trying to make or emphasize their point and have no idea of how to do this in a less flagrant or offensive manner. So what we appear to be observing, and discussing in this section, goes far beyond the pale of females piecing their ears for earrings or some sailor with a tattoo saying *"Mother."* It is now the soul or personality of the individual speaking something about them self that they have a need for the world to see and know no other way to express it.

Since most of us have many parts to our personalities and many thoughts we think about ourselves, it is reasonable to postulate that if this is one of our most effective forms of communications, that we will continue to utilize it until we learn something better or more efficient. So culturally speaking, we may see this behavior of cutting or etching and piercing on the increase for the foreseeable future.

In the case of females receiving tattoos to intimate parts of the body I have been told that they regard the tattoo artist (usually a male) as a professional in much the same way as they regard a physician. This is possibly denial. The reality is that most body art to "intimate" body parts is there to promote sensuality and sexuality. So the question arises; how can anyone expect the tattoo provider to divest themselves of their sexual desires and still perform the sexual tattoo art at his or her best? For the process understandably is usually a collaboration of the tattoo recipient and the tattoo provider. The reality here seems more likely to be that the recipient is actually paying someone to have sexual (or near sexual) admittance to his or her intimate body part(s). To the (visual) male that she is now or will be dating in the future this is an obvious unavoidable reminder that someone else has seen and handled those intimate areas before him. So now what you may have is a subtle covert issue of mistrust becoming a foundational part of the relationship. Yet most family and marriage therapist will attest that it is trust which is the bedrock or foundational part of any successful marital relationship. Of course in the interest of not being seen as prudish or out of touch, he will usually say nothing negative. He may even convince himself consciously that this means nothing. But on some level it has to register. And in someway it must affect his behavior toward her. Maybe that behavior is simply to avoid marriage. Or even in marriage a lingering doubt as to her complete fidelity may always be present but repressed, and may become manifested in irrational behavior that appears totally unconnected to what is viewed by many as a relatively insignificant act. But whatever the case I believe that this is one of the major reasons that underlie the debate on whether or not tattoos are a sign of promiscuity in females.

All that said, I will attempt to address the most relative questions concerning this behavior, such as: why is it that more and more young people seem to be lacking the ability to define or express themselves succinctly and politely with their voices? And why must they seek approval from the world around them? These are usually the kind of needs that are met within the boundaries of the family social unit. Self expression and the act of defining oneself in terms that don't call for permanent marks on or holes through the skin, or profanity is usually modeled in the family social unit. But when the family social unit cannot supply this esteem and/or modeling of behavior we will still find a way to express who we are to those about us. We have a healthy need to be noticed within the boundaries of a balanced and functional family social unit.

Other Psychological Factors

1. *Personality disorders:* Officially a personality disorder is defined as, *"An enduring pattern of inner experience and behavior that deviates markedly for the expectations of the individual's culture... The enduring pattern is inflexible and pervasive across a broad range of personal and social situations.. "* This dysfunctional pattern of behavior influences how the individual thinks, feels, interacts and reacts to others, and how well the are able to control their impulses.

   The general cause for these disorders is best explained by the *theory of Functional Biology.* This is when "predisposing biology combines with disruptive early experience(s) to create disorder that then becomes permanent brain wiring." In other words the same way that the body can have a tendency towards certain diseases or ailments, so can the mind. For example, those in your family may have a very high tendency toward skin cancer But unlike your siblings you have always worn the proper clothing and right type of sunscreen to protect yourself. Some of them later develop skin cancer and you do not. That is explainable. But then one of your first cousins that has the same family biological predisposition and has also took the same proper precautions as you develop skin cancer. This is a little more difficult to explain.

So, though there are times when you both need biological and social/environmental factors to set of a physical condition, sometimes that condition can be set of by only one of these factors, seemingly independent of the other. This is true also for mental or psychological conditions.

For the sake of discussion think of a personality as a pie of relatively equal slices. Now picture that same pie with some of the slices missing. In a fruit pie nothing happens. But in the personality pie you get overcompensation. The slices that are there tend to overextend themselves to make up for the missing slices. So what you wind up with instead of a relatively emotionally balanced individual is someone prone to a notable variety of extremes depending on their specific disorder or disorders.

The two most prevalent types of personality disorders, or at least the most dangerous, that I have encountered when working with adolescents and adults in forensics are those of *Conduct Disorder* for adolescents and *Antisocial Personality Disorder* for adults. They are essentially the same pathologically, so basically what we are speaking about is chronology or time. Clinically, the adolescent has not had these behavioral patterns long enough to be considered a true sociopath.

A close look at some of the major symptoms of these disorders will explain not only their prevalence but also their basis for being so pronounced within this population.

1. *Generally, an ongoing or sustained pattern of disregard for the rights of others:* I do not believe that sympathy and empathy are necessarily innate to humans but are taught to us early on through the parent-child bonding process and the examples set by our early primary care givers. We in turn are then taught how to apply these concepts first to

other family members and then later to those in our society. It is in the bonding process that we first experience our feelings of security and comfort. But in the absence of this security or examples of kindness to others, we are left with the very strong instinct of survival or self-preservation.

There is also something else worth mentioning here which is a part of early childhood development known as *egocentrism.* This is when as very young children we believe that the world revolves around us. This maybe characterized in situations like when a child goes running to their mother after a scuffle with a playmate crying and saying, *"He hit me!"* And if mom did not witness the event she may ask who it was that hit him or her only to hear the same response again this time with a greater emphasis on *"HE."* In the child's mind the parent should know who *"HE"* is, because naturally everything revolves around him or her. We should lose or at least begin to moderate this perspective of life by the time we leave concrete thinking, begin to mature, and become able to think in abstract and altruistic terms, which would normally be somewhere around 11-12 years of age. But what happens when someone doesn't mature psychosocially as they should? This is known as at least one form of *cognitive repression.* Someone stuck or failing to advance in thinking in comparison to most others their age in society.

You see, much of how we mature psychosocially is obtained by watching others and by applying socially acceptable principles, many times through trial and error, to successfully negotiate life. This is part and parcel of the process of social and psychological maturation. However, if someone doesn't have healthy examples in their lives, they will inevitably observe and imitate unhealthy behavior and negotiate life vis-a-vis this dysfunctional conduct. Instead of using healthy decision making to solve problems in their lives they may turn to the use of drugs to create fantasy worlds where the problem either doesn't exist or at least is no longer viewed with the same urgency. Or they may turn to crime to solve their problems. Many turn to both.

As a therapist it has been my experience that whatever age at which the client began using these methods to negotiate life is the cognitive and psychological age at which they will often enter therapy. Regardless of their chronological age, if they began using these destructive methods of problem solving at age 12 and they are now age 30, they will likely present in perception and behavior as a 12 year old. That is the point where they ceased to psychosocially mature. So they often haven't the faintest idea of how a socially healthy adult would address some of the very same problems they face. Also if and when such a solution is presented to them, they are often unwilling to put it into practice because most of our problems are not acquired or solved overnight. So the immediate gratification thinking that is connected to this lifestyle will not allow for solutions that won't fit this basic criterion. Crime and drugs do fit.

2. *Specific Symptoms:* When you couple the lack of proper parental bonding with cognitive repression, what you get is a very self-centered individual that still thinks and behaves in very immature and often dangerous patterns of behavior. You essentially have someone with the physical prowess and desires of an adult but the mentality of a child - a child that has not been taught to extend empathy or sympathy beyond self and maybe, *maybe*, immediate relatives or possibly to some that they have bonded with in other fashions such as the extreme physical and emotional hazing that can occur during some initiations.

So regardless what this personality disorder has been motivated or caused by it will show up in an individual as some or all of the following: *a) Someone who fails to conform to social norms with respect to lawful behavior, b) Deceitfulness as indicated by repeated lying, c) impulsiveness or failure to plan ahead d) irritability and aggressiveness, d) reckless disregard for the safety of self or others, consistent irresponsibility, and e) lack of remorse.* For someone to be considered a true *antisocial* all they have to do is consistently display three or more of these specific criteria. They would also have had to be displaying some of this behavior prior to age 15, and they could not just be happening with respect to another disorder such as schizophrenia. And remember, they must be 18 or older. When you see the same behavioral pattern in those younger than 18, it is often called *conduct disorder.*

Everyone that works in the lower echelons of Food Service doesn't have a personality disorder. But of those that I have worked with, especially adolescent and young adults, this particular personality disorder appears to be increasing. And what I have tried to present in this section to you the reader is a professional opinion that seeks to explain it.

Finally, I would like to point out that with any personality disorder someone can have the full blown disorder where many of the symptoms are observed and sustained over a long period of time, or may merely display *traits* of the disorder. This is where symptoms appear with less frequency and are accompanied by less extreme behaviors and/or acts towards others.

Intervention at the onset of symptoms or traits of a disorder is always better than waiting to see if and when a full blown disorder will appear.

I would also not wish to gloss over the element of *conscious choice* in the antisocial, sociopath, or psychopathic mindset. What we are ultimately speaking about is behavior. And regardless of the underlying or precipitating factors, behavior can be modified or totally eradicated and replaced. That it is not easy or is extremely difficult in many cases is a given. But human beings are not just domesticated animals. There is no evidence that even remotely suggests that *Fido or Fluffy* have ever been seen looking into the night skies and wondering *"why am I here?"* We humans can not only think, but we can think about our thoughts. This gives us the unique ability to examine our own thought processes and make adjustments as we see fit. Of those who wish change, they may choose from a variety of interventions. Some choose the will, some psychotherapy, while others choose a religious or spiritual intervention. And still some choose to combine two or more of these interventions to produce the change they choose to make in their approach to life.

The problem with behavior is that even dysfunctional behavior can become comfortable, or more accurately, comfortably known to us. And we seem to have an innate resistance to change coupled with a fear of the unknown. So because we can become comfortable with most all behaviors, functional or dysfunctional, we tend to naturally resist any efforts to modify or eradicate them because this forces us out of our comfort zones and into the unknown. Even when we are aware that such behavior is in direct opposition to existing laws or societal norms with regard to our expected treatment of others, often we persist.

2. *Conspicuous consumption:* The term was originated by Thorstien Veblen an American economist and social scientist in his first publication, *The Theory of the Leisure Class* (1899). He theorized, after clinical observation of the ways some wealthy elite provocatively displayed and consumed material

gain, their reasoning for this gaudy show of affluence. He noted concerning the desire for conspicuous consumption: "part of the attraction of the good is simply its high price." For the sake of our study though, it is a much deeper matter than that of elitism or economic one-upmanship. I will take this attraction of and desire to display costly material goods a step further, into the realm of value systems.

It has been my observation that humans invariably have two types of basic value systems. Simply stated, this system is the portion of the personality or psychological make up of the individual by which they define their own worthiness. These two types of value systems are ***Internal*** and ***External***.

Individuals that have an ***internal value system*** are able to look inside themselves with typical introspection and take inventory of relationships and accomplishments that provides them with a sense of their worth or worthiness. Internal value systems appear innate but must be reinforced and affirmed by individuals we respect and esteem. The elements of that value system must also be accepted and affirmed by the greater society. For it is in macro-society where the *laws of the land* for legal and acceptable conduct is established. It is also the function of macro-society to define what is either socially revered or reviled. We all seem to look inwardly for our value system at first. We appear to be wired this way. But what happens when an individual looks inwardly and only sees negatives? E.g. suppose there is this nagging sense that we should be farther along in school or in life than we are. Suppose looking inwardly we are not able to find any pluses in our list of worthwhile personal accomplishments? In fact, compared to individuals our age in the greater society, we may inwardly feel that we stack up as abysmal failures. For even when living in a very closed clique or sub-culture we cannot escape the images and values of macro-society. We see commercials on television. We pass billboards. We attend schools etc. And while our closed groups may affirm antisocial behavior we cannot escape the stark contrast between where we are and where society has ascribed we should be. At this point introspection likely becomes too painful an exercise.

Yet we must all operate with some value system that makes us feel worthy, that gives us the level that our psyche requires. I believe this is when the individual forces their view outwardly to construct an ***external value system***. However, unlike its internal counterpart it is not based on positive accomplishments and affirmations of acceptance by the majority of society at large, but based on possession and control of material things and even individuals in their proximity. Conspicuous consumption now becomes an integral part of the lifestyle of the individual. He will control as many and as much as he can and show those around him how successful he is at this by his outward trappings. You may wonder why some drug dealers would wear and drive the very things that place them under suspicion for being a drug dealer. Or why some pimps or madams would do the same thing. All these individuals face arrest and jail or prison time if caught at their crimes. And they do get caught. So why send out the very visual signals that will cue the authorities to observe you as a person of interest? Sometimes answering a question with another question seems appropriate. And I believe the better question here is also our answer in brief. How do you ask someone to abandon his or her value system whether internal or external?

3. **The Pride Incongruity:** When a therapist describes someone's affect as being incongruent it means that the client is presenting (arriving into a counseling session) with a facial expression, appearance, or demeanor that is drastically different than their current known or implied emotional state. For instance, a hospitalized rape victim who is laughing and telling jokes during the initial interview in the sexual trauma ward, or a client describing their recent witnessing of the horrific murder

of their mother at the hands of their father who tells the story with blank expression and devoid of tears. In other words there is a stark contrast between the emotional state that the individual shows to others and what is actually happening in that person's present life or recent past.

In 1968 there was a song that went, *"Say it loud, I'm black and I'm proud."* And for certain there is nothing wrong in taking pride in one's race in much the same manner one might take pride in ones faith or personal appearance. These are all elements or parts of the complete individual and deserve care and consideration.

But what good is pride or more specifically, a proud look when your life is a wreck? And what I am about to say I do so with the utmost of care and concern. But anything less than directness here can leave room for ambiguity, and ambiguity will not allow for the clear connection that needs to be made between behavior, consequence, and appropriate response to consequence. It is the appropriateness of our responses to the consequences of our behavior that indicates learning, specifically behavior that is self destructive in nature. Conversely, inappropriate responses tend to be indicative of a lack of learning. Therefore the negative behavior will likely be repeated.

Take a trip with me to a local microcosm. Visit many urban area malls in this country on a Saturday evening and you will see an abundance of young people, African-Americans included. Many will be dressed in designer named clothing and shoes and a large number of females will have designer purses and professionally done nails and hairstyles. They also are likely to have the necessary jewelry, body piercing, and tattoos that show they "belong." All this will probably be accompanied by the newest brands of cellular phones.

I am aware that most or all of this is done in connections with the rituals and discoveries of youth. I am not trying to dissuade healthy youthful exuberance or deny the power connected to fads in order to conform to and identify with their fellows, but keep in mind what we are talking about here is incongruent affect connected to the current factors of someone's life. That being said and noting the alarming statistics for young African Americans for unwed births, abortions, sexually transmitted diseases, violent and drug related juvenile histories, and poor tests scores, several questions come to mind. But primarily the most profound of these questions should focus on behavior versus expressions. This is the incongruity, simply asked in these questions. Why all the smiles, the laughter, and the levity that is often accompanied by proud looks that border on arrogance? Are they not aware of the social cancers that are eating away at their own ethnic and age group? Or are they aware and just don't care, because we have failed them in terms of not just teaching this information but also emphasizing it's gross impact on us as a people and as a nation? Are we zealously advocating for their well being by not only pointing out consequences, but also guarding against assisting or enabling them to repeat self-destructive behavior by holding them accountable in terms of those consequences?

Obviously and thankfully the aforementioned disturbing statistics do not apply to all African American adolescents or young adults. But the concern is that the numbers who they do apply to are significant and increasing.

This incongruity seems to also be culturally pervasive. Never have so many African Americans been so affluent. We have more black business owners and millionaires than at any other time in the history of our nation. And this affluence and notoriety adorns us in much the same way as the decorative jewelry and designer clothing adorns the aforementioned mall youths. The popular magazine covers both ethnic and mainstream give the appearance that all is well and getting better. This is an illusion and totally disconnected from the reality of the situation.

I will agree that opportunities abound as never before for all Americans, but this fact cannot begin to offset the astronomical problems facing African Americans in particular. We are literally responsible for our own possible genocide. Many of our youth that make it past our high infant mortality rates and abortions are murdering each other over little or nothing. Family News In Focus on their January 18th 2008 broadcast reported that in just 3 days more African Americans lives will be terminated through abortion than the historical total of all those who ever lost their lives at the hands of the Klan. The happy and proud looks, the shiny apparel, and the nice cars betray the truth of a desperate non-conflict. I say non-conflict because we do not appear to be struggling to survive as a people. We seem to be more interested in surviving as selfish, self-righteous individuals who lack the ability to feel compassion for anything or anyone outside of our own closed circles. But in much the same way that America cannot survive an attack unless her citizens survive African Americans cannot survive this self-inflicted assault unless we also survive as a community.

Any African American that stands idly and selfishly by only to watch us implode in on ourselves as a race without doing all that he or she can to halt and turn this around is the truest and most profound of incongruities: a person without a people.

4. *Recessive behavioral decline:* Left uncorrected, behavior will degrade at a rate proportionate to its lack of restraints or correctives. In other words, the less negative behavior is addressed, the quicker its downward spiral. Negative or destructive behavior is also communicable. So this decline or degradation can happen on a horizontal basis where it affects

others *contemporarily*, and it can also happen vertically where it will affect those who are to come in the future and can be expressed in terms of a *generational* decline. E.g. Schools or other institutions that fail to consistently enforce established standards of conduct will almost certainly see a rise in behavioral problems with two basic groups of students. Those who are presently enrolled because, a significant portion of whom behavior will be negatively impacted due to the "one bad apple" effect, and those who will enroll at later dates because the old level of rebellion will itself have become the norm and will likely be seen as archaic and restrictive to the new arrivals.

As the number of African American children born to single mothers increase so do the obvious behavioral problems, especially those problems connected to violence and sexual promiscuity. The children in these households are now having children themselves. They are also becoming grandparents at early ages. The behavioral problems directly associated with their lack of a balanced family and the teaching of appropriate interpersonal and societal boundaries is now being passed on to new generations in whom the problems will certainly worsen. The parent cannot pass on to the child what they themselves have not learned and do not know.

The most sobering factor in all of this is the question - Where will African Americans be as a culture in two or three of these rather short generations? The generations will be short because you have adolescent parents reproducing other adolescent parents. So whatever the ultimate destructive and catastrophic effect of this rather rapid behavioral decline on the African American race, it may culminate not in the 40 to 60 years which might usually describe 2-3 generations, but possibly in 20 to 30 years.

5. ***Learned behavior and change:*** Behavioral change in a home environment can be very similar to change in a clinical environment. Since much of this treatise is devoted to the home or family environment, I will briefly describe the solicitation of change in a professional environment based on the approach that I personally utilize in much of my work. I do so because there are principles that are also applicable to the family setting.

As a licensed mental health professional, of course I should be able to readily identify to anyone who asks what my approach to psychotherapy is. So for the record, my preferred approach is *cognitive behavioral therapy.* Simply put, this is a form of therapy that focuses most on thoughts and observable behavior as opposed to those therapies rooted in the realm of emotions or affect. And as a behaviorist, most times I am at best only mildly concerned about what someone's motivation is for behavioral change. If you are a therapist, consider what I'm going to say. If you are not a therapist, some of the basic premise of what I am about to say may also be useful to you.

When working with someone with the goal of assisting that person with behavioral change never be afraid to harness any desire or motivation that is going in your direction. That is, if the destination or goal of that desire or motive is ultimately the betterment of the client and does no harm to others, then use it to your advantage. For example, if in the winter the sole motivation for someone living on the streets to self-admit into a homeless recovery program is to not be cold, that's ok. They may not be interested in recovery, vocational assistance, or therapy at the time. They are not yet thinking on that level, only on the level of basic survival. But because they are now in a program where structure, responsibility, and accountability exists, it will likely force them into functioning mentally on a higher level than they may have in years. Then you will begin to see at least the capacity for change begin to show itself. You will see it in their eyes and in their attitudes. You will hear it in their voices. But it will still be up to you to capitalize on this *awakening* by requiring and affirming new patterns of behavior.

And by the way, *"faking it until you make it"* is also okay. Behavior, even feigned behavior, if repeated often enough becomes learned behavior. If someone is just going through the motions to avoid uncomfortable consequences like being cold, that's fine. Have them to keep going through the motions. One day it will become second nature to just go through the motions. And change will have happened before your very eyes, and theirs.

Is it really that simple you ask? When a professional or a parent is committed to consistency it is often just that simple; not easy, just not complicated. That's why I'm a behaviorist.

6. **Rejected social tenets:** There are usually only three reasons why children seem to reject incorporating the value system and moral constructs of their parents or those with authority over them. *(1) Hypocrisy (2) Harm and (3) Devaluation.*

   1. *Hypocrisy-* Like it or not there is such a thing as *moral authority.* This is the basis that gives us the right, aside from position, to hold others accountable. But moral authority, unlike *positional authority*, cannot be given or bestowed upon someone by virtue of rank or positional standing. It must be earned by example. When we lack moral authority to bring others into accountability because our own lives do not reflect the very standard(s) we are insisting or requiring of them, we will often be viewed as hypocritical. And rejection of those standards will come as soon as the ones they are being forced upon become or perceive themselves able to mount any impressionable resistance.

In the case of children detecting this hypocrisy in their parent(s) or other authority figures in their lives, the age of the child is a major factor. Some children begin to think abstractly very early while most children begin in late childhood or early adolescence. Hypocrisy is an abstract concept. The concrete thinking of early childhood will usually not fully comprehend this concept, and so it will be much easier for authority figures to utilize the *"do as I say, not as I do approach"* with some degree of success. However it is important to remember that values manifest themselves in behavior and children of all ages observe the behavior of those around them, especially care givers, authority figures, and peers. So in that sense "values are more caught than taught." Yet during the formative years from infancy to childhood, parents may get away with behavior that is not congruent with what they are requiring from those their children. As stated beforehand, hypocrisy is an abstract concept and the child, even though puzzled as he or she may be, may not grasp that concept when they are being disciplined or called into account for repeating behavior that they have observed in their parents.

Understandably there will be behaviors that parents will be able to participate in that children will not for a variety of reasons such as age, strength, intellectual maturity and others. But all those kinds of behaviors and the reasons for their prohibitions to children are fairly easy to explain when the child reaches the age when they pose the question of "why is this allowed for you and not me" and they <u>will</u> reach that age. This is not the type behavior we are focusing on. The kind of behavior in question here is the type of behavior that violates the basic morality or rules structure of the family social unit, rules such as those prohibiting lying when the child routinely hears parents lie to their bosses about their health, to bill collectors about finances, or to friends they don't want to speak to on the phone or see at the moment to name a few.

The child's age when he or she is first able to fully perceive this paradoxical behavior in the parent is an important factor, because it is highly probable that it is also the age when their resentment over this hypocrisy will begin to fester. They will suddenly realize that the parent is subjecting them to that which they will not subject them self to. And barring a correction in the parent's behavior, this resentment will likely continue to swell until it begins to surface in adverse, rebellious, and possibly violent behavior. Not all this negative energy will always be rooted in anger either. Much of it will often be rooted in the sadness and disappointment involved in the loss of innocence - the loss of all or a significant portion of the image the child has of the parent.

The younger the child is when this realization first occurs the longer they have to seethe with this emotional turmoil before it finally crescendos in the final act of breakaway rebellion where they reject the authority of the parent absolutely and lastingly.

2. *Harm* – If the child perceives either through his or her own experience or through information from another source that the family social tenets are harming them or some other vulnerable member of the family unit, this may also be reason enough for the rejection of that unit's basic social tenets. But this is not always the case. For instance in the case of abuse (physical, sexual, or emotional), a child will likely at some juncture realize at least some of the harm that this behavior is

causing them. They may even promise themselves never to do the same when they become adults with families, only to repeat the same behaviors when they indeed do become adults.

There are several serious psychological reasons for the re-manifestation of this behavior in the adult victim. One reason in general is because it is difficult for most of us to get past the learning of our formative years. More specifically, I believe that one obvious and overlooked reason for this is because though the behavior was abusive to them, it was also presented by the abusing parent (or other authority figure) as a problem solving mechanism. In the case of physical abuse, it may have been falsely represented as legitimate corporal punishment. In the case of sexual abuse, it may have been falsely represented as a way to show legitimate love. In the case of pure emotional abuse that is manifested e.g. in parental detachment, it may have been falsely represented as assisting the child to become more mature and independent.

And so years later when the child who is now an adult is faced with a situation that is problematic for them and they have been taught no other technique for solving it, they will likely resort to the only method(s) that they have been taught. It is a "known" and it is therefore more comfortable to practice the known than to leave the unfamiliar grounds of the comfort zone and learn new behavior. They may have also bought into the lie or misrepresentation of the abusive behavior as legitimate to assist them through denial or suppression to disconnect from their own inner pain and turmoil. Whatever the case, taking personal responsibility for change is often difficult and painful. Sometimes sound professional help is required, but even that must be a personal choice.

In the case where the adult victim actually rejects the abusive or harmful family social tenet, they do so ostensibly because they have not bought into the lie or misrepresentation. For whatever reason they have been able to see the behavior for the abuse or harm that it is and has likely had access to other non-pathological methods for producing or promoting healthier states and balance within the family and themselves.

3. *Devaluation* – There maybe times when social tenets are devalued because those in authority have been hypocritical or harmful in their approach to setting and maintaining the moral and behavioral standards of the family social unit. However, there will also be times when those standards will be rejected solely because individuals, for the most part, are usually sentient possessors of their own wills. We have the ability to weigh the circumstances and make our own choices. Caring parents and other authority figures routinely blame themselves when a child or someone who has been in their charge goes awry in their behavior. Time and time again they may replay their rearing or training of the individual to see where they may have gone wrong in their relationship or authoritative role with them. And while it is good to evaluate ones own performance in any process, it is counter productive to live with the guilt of something you may not be responsible for at all. Parents are not perfect. And if you have been honest with your child concerning your imperfections, admitted to your known mistakes, usually "practiced what you preached," it is my opinion that your guilt is probably undeserved.

Sometimes your children simply place less value on your approach to living than on one they have personally contrived or observed in others. For instance, parents with multiple children may have strong work ethics. In a perfect world it would be reasonable to assume that their children will also have the same strong work ethic. However, in the real world this is not always the case. Yes, most of the children will probably have this trait but there is always the reality that some will not. And a child can come to the conclusion that the workaday world is not for them for a variety of reasons. They may have peers whose opinions they value more and so influence them to think differently of the tenets of their own family social unit. They may have become *criminal or irresponsible thinkers* (learn more about this in chapter IV **Criminal Intent**). This is where the child makes a conscious choice to begin thinking, and subsequently developing a pattern of behavior driven by this thinking, that in time will bring them into direct conflict with the law or with other forms of authority.

The point is that the devaluation of social tenets is usually a matter of choice that individuals make for reasons that often have very little to do with anything other than what they believe works best for them. Many times with thinking autonomous human beings it is just that simple.

In such cases, parents still maintain the prime responsibility of being consistent in their observance and application of family social tenets. However, please do not confuse consistency with inflexibility. Learning in a family unit is not exclusive to children and the children of the family can also do teaching, though primary to adults. They can, when allowed and encouraged, introduce new healthy and functional perspectives for overall betterment of the family social unit. For instance they may suggest that family meetings (where applicable) not always be chaired by the same individual(s). This would be a golden opportunity for everyone to learn the rules on how to conduct a meeting. And it could also cut down on possible boredom and the connotation that a family meeting means that someone (usually the same individual) will do the "preaching" and everyone else has to just sit and suffer through it.

Parents are not to be flexible however when such ideas and/or behaviors that are clearly harmful and dysfunctional are being adopted by their progeny and seeking entrance into the established family social tenets. Adults cannot observe children 24 hours a day nor under normal circumstances should they. But when possible, parents should always insist that family social tenets be adhered to. Parents should not be afraid to say "no." A "no" decision should be one that reflects concern, be based in logic, and also easily explainable when it is necessary and convenient to do so. But a parent should never bow to outside pressure to abandon his or her principle. As children, most of us either have or will violate the rules or social tenets of our family at some point in time. When this happens, the child should always be reminded (even if it is after the fact) that they have violated parental teaching. If a child has received consistent and loving discipline, this violation will bother their conscience, and that will greatly assist in correcting or abandoning harmful behavior.

But when parents have been overly pliable and grossly inconsistent, the converse is also true. Children are likely to repeat and increase harmful behavior to highly destructive levels. Such situations are prime examples of social tenets being devalued because they are gelatinous and murky. When peers or the child's own experiences present a tenet that is more clearly defined and consistent, even if it is ultimately harmful, the child may place more value on it merely because it is a known that they can depend on.

7. **Malignant inclinations:** We have a tendency to devour our own. When I first became a professional I fully expected at least some of the problems that I received from whites. I did not say that they weren't emotionally troubling me, only that at some level I expected some of it. But in all fairness, many more whites assisted and befriended me than those who sought to harm me.

But where I was caught by surprise was from the level of animosity and virulence directed at me by many of my own race. It is not that I hadn't seen this when I was growing up, but that was the late sixties and early to mid seventies. Those were different times. We were just beginning to iron out the kinks of the newfound freedom associated with the Civil Rights movement and the general cultural upheaval of the sixties generation. I went to college and graduate school both as an adult with a fair amount of living under my belt, so by the time I got to the job market as a professional, I imagined much of the old mentality connected to racial self-hatred and jealousy of achievers among us to have eased or dissipated some, at least from the workplace where we are always under open scrutiny. Not so... This cancer was not even in partial remission.

As the only African American male professional in many of the divisions or departments I was assigned to, I was not only spurned by other professionals I worked with but even by cleaning people assigned to clean our offices. African American males and female janitorial staff would routinely skip my office while cleaning the offices of whites along with African American female co-workers. One female janitor was so resistant to the idea of cleaning my office she told a lie on me (claiming I had screamed at her my request to have my trash emptied) to justify her actions to her superior to whom I complained. Fortunately my supervisor, when he was contacted said that her report was totally uncharacteristic of me and that he did not believe it. A female co-worker also was witness to my conversation with the janitorial staffer and said that she would provide corroboration if needed.

African American cafeteria workers would routinely display no courtesy to me as I went through the lunch lines and nearly always provided me with noticeably smaller portions than those on either side of me who were usually whites and African American females. This behavior went on until once again, I had to speak with the cafeteria manager. He had to see it for himself to believe it.

When my career reached its management phase, most of the resistance and obstacles that I experienced in making my departments' successes were from other African Americans, both on my staff and in the layer of management above me. Most of my staff I was always able to win over once they saw that my only motive was improvement for them as clinicians and to our department as service providers. But without exception, I was never able to win over those African American managers above me. They would at times; become very bold in their vehemence, obviously believing they could act without impunity. After awhile they laid subterfuge aside and openly sought to initiate my professional demise within the agency.

I have had orders to my staff countermanded in my absence. I have had trap meetings that were no more than frame-ups to take the fall poor decisions made by those above me. The list goes on. And as I have stated, it is not that I haven't had white manager above me attempt some of the same things, but it has been attempted far more often by African Americans who have without a doubt been the more Machiavellian of the two. Ironically enough, many times it has been white executives above them who had to investigate and evaluate the situation, and effect some sort of direct and drastic intervention to make them stand down.

Now my undergraduate degree is in Vocational Education. I was also an electrical technician aboard nuclear submarines in the Navy. I was taught in those curricula of study that when something goes wrong with a classroom or a piece of operational equipment, the first place to look for errors is with self. So in all or most of the instances I've mentioned (and there are far too many more to recount here) I did just that. I monitored my attitude and affect to make sure they were friendly and my words respectful and courteous. And since none of the people that I mentioned ever spoke to or greeted me unless I spoke to or greeted them, I tried to always take the initiative in this. Doing this changed nothing. In fact, it became the expectation that I would be the one to speak, and the times that I may have been preoccupied or just tired of this process and said or did nothing, things got worse.

Speaking with other African American male professionals, I have found that my experiences are not unique. Many (not all) had similar experiences from time to time in the workplace, in church, and in social as well as family settings. But the personal level is not the only level on which this dilemma manifests itself. It can also be seen culturally.

Individuals and groups that purport to lead and watch out for African Americans are not producing good results overall, and this should be evident to the most casual observer. Many of these individuals and groups or agencies are funded via public donations and/or governmental grants. Some have and are continuing to do a good service, but in my opinion, they are the exception and not the rule. Many have been around for decades and have simply learned how to produce the numbers on paper or say the right words in the public arena that will categorize them as having either successfully met grant funding requirements or furthered the interest of their supporters. The only problem with this is that in the real world, away from the paperwork and the microphones, we are going to hell in a hand basket.

The truth is that they are largely ineffective but are unwilling get out of the way. Among them the argument hardly ever seems to be about who is actually helping or not helping, but from what I have seen, it is most often about turf. Populations and constituencies are divided and fought over among them much in the same manner that drug dealers and pimps fight over street corners. But why shouldn't that be the case, if you are after the same things as dealers and pimps? Money, recognition, control and first and foremost repeat business. It is the customer or client who keeps coming back that is the mainstay of *all these enterprises*.

What we actually have here, both at the personal and cultural levels, is what is commonly referred to as the "crabs in a bucket" syndrome. Being from a coastal region of the county, I've had many occasions to witness the following example used in this analogy. If you've ever watched freshly caught crabs in a bucket or basket, they can be their own worst enemies in regard to escaping their prison. For as soon as one crab reaches for the rim of the container a second or third crab reaches hold of him and tries to pull them self up over the first fellow. What ultimately results is that often they all fall back into the container only to repeat the process over and over again. Even after becoming weak due to oxygen deprivation they still clamp down and hold on to each other in vice like grips. It is as though as their last act they have committed to ensuring that no one among them succeeds in leaving their container.

Not to excuse this mentality, only to explain it, I suspect much of it has been conditioned into us in much the same manner that the slave era mentality almost permeates our entire American culture. That is, we remain more divided along racial lines than by anything else. It is the prime mover in where most of us live, worship, and with whom we form close relationships and ultimately marry. I believe this is largely a hold over from Pre-Civil War America. And I can firmly support my hypothesis on the matter and will attempt to do so in my follow-up to this particular work. In this work however, I have only touched on this point to illustrate the conditioning coming from that era, as it is pertinent to African American culture today.

In Pre-Civil War America slaves, could often outnumber their owners on any given estate. So slavery proponents had to figure out ways once they had purchased their "property" of keeping them in check and under their control. Chains and shackles were not useful in fields and performing other forms of manual labor. Obviously whites were armed and slaves were not, but that only addressed the physical environment - and only partialy I might add because in the real world the physical environment is often dynamic with the ability to change at any given time. Nightfall, where visibility was minimal, always came. Even in daylight hours slaves often worked performing field and yard work where simple foliage, vegetation, and architectural structures could obscure the vision of their captors at any time. There was a dire need for another type of control to be implemented, a control that could even respond to gaps in physical security. And there was.

This control was implemented at the psychological level. We were actually turned against each other by slave owners through what could be loosely described as the promotion process. When certain slaves would be granted positions over others the expectation was obviously not that their primary allegiance be to their fellow slaves, but rather to their owners. Since these positions probably were accompanied with their own perks they were to be coveted and protected. This would of course mean hampering or completely eliminating any competition. And that competition would naturally come from the pool comprised of fellow slaves. Also, the practice by some of these individual of staying in the "master's" good graces by divulging information on other blacks concerning planned escapes or revolts was also not unheard off in this era.

This malignancy has gone nowhere. Today in rhetoric and dialogue we often identify whites as the cause of many of the problems that minorities face in our contemporary culture. Yet in practical behavior we African Americans conduct ourselves as though it is the achievers among us who are our worst enemies. Those blacks who still ascribe to very high standards of education and hold their children to them, or who still believe in knowing your job just as well or better than anyone else, and who still believe that their nation is worth defending are becoming an anomaly. They are often held up for ridicule and targeted for demise not just by a few prejudice whites but by many bitter and jealous African Americans.

CHAPTER III
The Community and Macro-Social Aspects
(A complicit culture)

It is understood that the individual is ultimately responsible for choices and behavior. However most of us don't live to ourselves or in a vacuum. The community at large can be a catalyst for growth or decline in the individual and in families. If we are to address and hopefully solve the problem of the breakdown of African American families, which obviously affects us all, we must first acknowledge the part that society (the general and current culture) plays in the lives of families especially those more highly at risk.

The general culture must stop its role in the demise of our nation as a whole, especially and with more rapidity, the African American family social unit. Athletes guilty of crimes and/or extremely violent and provocative behavior are rewarded even at the college level with increase in attention, adulation, and many times more income. The news media should stop giving notable coverage and air time only to those blacks in leadership roles that ascribe to their particular social and political preferences. News networks and programs are not talk shows; they are the *news*. Those in media must cover different perspectives on approaching social problems with some degree of objectivity if a comprehensive approach to these issues is ever to have measurable results in our times. They have the power to help or to hinder.

Sex is rampant among adolescents. Hollywood and the public schools in particular are not helping the problem when they fight tooth and nail against abstinence based programs, thereby convincing young people that it is almost impossible to wait until after marriage before engaging in sexual activity. This ideology is dangerous and reflects very little faith in their ability to do anything except act upon their baser drives and urges. We set them up for failure. Hollywood has been aware for some time that family oriented films with more traditional themes that contain less nudity, profanity and violence are almost always box office magic; but they appear highly reticent to increase the production of them at any pace other than that of a slow crawl.

I ask in all honesty and candor: where is the evidence that this approach or mindset is working for the culture as a whole or specifically for African American families? The truth of the matter is that we will never be able to fix this horrendous problem unless the culture at some level cooperates. Movie and music companies executives need to begin to question their peers about their responsibility to the public, as should some journalist and those involved in athletics at every level. Someone somewhere in government needs to see the sheer destruction involved in a long term approach to assistance that deprives the individual of the struggle we all need intrinsically to do and become our best. No one with a dependent, hand out mentality ever achieved greatness or independence while continuing in that mindset. Does anyone care that they might be complicit in debilitating and destroying a people?

The culture is also complicit because it sets out to destroy anyone who disagrees with it. The major players and forces that are becoming wealthy via the very demise of our country and its most vulnerable and at risk citizens will spare no cost in seeking to besmirch, lambaste, and harm those who seek to help those in jeopardy because it is interfering with their own income and/or influence.

Other institutions, attitudes, and trends in the community also affect this decline, and some time is given in the following pages to address what I view as a few of the most prevalent. Some of these forces may be the product and natural results of our desire to be benevolent as a nation. Others are the result of greed and pathology. But they all deserve attention and the acknowledgement that they not only exist but greatly affect the direction of blacks in this country.

The Hispanic Question

I have heard the question asked, "What about the large number of Hispanics moving into these lower echelon jobs in foodservice and other industries? I thought that they were doing jobs that Americans refuse to do anymore?" Well first of all this doesn't appear to be the case. For example, Hispanics only represent approximately 25% of fruit pickers, positions that are often pointed to as an example of this. Second, we should acknowledge the reality that the largest segment of Hispanics coming into this country today are here illegally and provide a huge source of low skill, low wage labor that many businesses find hard to resist, as labor is most often the chief capital expenditure of business. Pair this with the fact that their illegal status makes it all the more likely that they will not complain to any noticeable degree about working conditions or pay, and it's a win-win scenario for the businesses that employ them. So the argument that illegal Hispanic immigrants are doing jobs that Americans will no longer do is far from accurate in many instances. It is just that with the lack of enforcement of existing laws that make it a crime to knowingly employ illegal aliens, employers in droves are making the choice to hire illegals in short because it improves their bottom line. Many of these same employers are also at the heart of legislation to grant illegals amnesty. Since Hispanics in large are not assimilating, a large segment of them are also not growing. They have high dropout rates, high crime statistics in many urban areas, and many are not learning the language. These are the kind of factors that will keep many Hispanics in these positions even if they are granted some form of amnesty. And at the same time it will take away any future chance of employers being charged for aiding and abetting if one day the authorities are ever pressured to uniformly enforce the existing immigration laws. So African Americans who remain at this low skill level will have ever increasing competition for even these jobs for the foreseeable future.

The illegal immigrants that appear to be benefiting most are those in the building and construction trades. Many started off in the lower paying positions, but they are now moving through them and becoming business owners themselves. They have come into these lower paid positions in the identical job markets as African Americans, but they come in with some major differences. Often they have an intact traditional family structure that is either present with them or they maintain regular communications with them along with the sharing of financial resources. So many of them are not only doing well, it is almost a guarantee that their children will do even better.

Most of us will admit (if we are honest) that the problems associated with illegal immigration are numerous and alarming. But illegal immigration is also a problem that our government seems to lack the will to deal effectively with for the present. Legislation that is being considered according to some like the Heritage Foundation will do very little to address the flow of illegals crossing U.S. borders. In the meantime, the current waves of immigrants, legal and illegal, coming to this country hasn't been seen in this proportion since the waves of European immigrants that came to these shores in the early parts of the last century. And yes, they definitely have among them those who seek only to over burden our criminal justice, medical, educational, and social welfare systems. But in contrast they also have among them many, like those former waves of Europeans, who have a strong sense of traditional family, a strong work ethic, and strong spiritual beliefs. I am not saying that European immigrants didn't engage in crime. They did. The list of gangsters, mobsters, and organized crime figures that were first and second generation European immigrants is lengthy. But thankfully they were not representative of the majority of legal European immigrants. Most Americans believe that immigration is good as long as it is legal because the first act of someone new to this nation should not be the commission of a crime.

That being said, in my observation Hispanic immigrants also display another asset to their sub-culture. They maintain much of their resources within their communities. A great deal of their shopping is accomplished with companies that employ other Hispanic immigrants. They save. When they purchase a vehicle and hire other workers usually it is from a pool of other Hispanics. They send funds outside the country in massive quantities to family members that are still in their native lands.

Consequently, I believe that a large portion of the earnings of their African American counterparts working in the same low tier jobs will leave their families and communities between 5pm Friday and 2am Sunday. A very large portion of those funds will likely be spent on music, beauty products and services, or funneled to purveyors of alcoholic beverages, cigarettes, sex clubs, pornography dealers, predatory lenders, etc. All these are legal within our society. And our nation is a free republic driven by a capitalist economic system and the "for profit" motive, all of which I strongly believe in. The one bright spot in all this is that those beauty products and services will be largely purchased from black owned businesses.

Notwithstanding, Monday morning will find many of these individuals and households divested of all, or near all, of some of the basic staples of life. There are no emergency fund savings. There is no over all gain of non-depreciable tangible assets. There is no budget for the coming week. There are no savings for education or eventual property ownership, both hallmarks of the American Dream. And widespread low credit scores will almost certainly rule out borrowing for any of the aforementioned without paying rates so exorbitant that "legalized usury" is the only term which accurately describe them.

One other note on this topic; during the mass European immigration of the last century our culture by its very structure demanded assimilation. The immigrant was required to adjust while not losing their own unique ethnic identity. They adjusted in terms of *language, law, and allegiance.* This served only to make us a stronger nation. So when war was thrust upon us we met the challenge as *one people*, with *one language, one law, and one allegiance.*

With the Hispanic migration however, this is not the case. Our action or lack of it on this problem is actually dividing us and making us weaker. Because we are no longer demanding assimilation we now have multiple languages with arguments over which one should be primary in any given circumstance. We have multiple applications of the law where illegal immigrants are not required to respect the same law as American citizens. And we have multiple allegiances as evidenced in part by the vast number of dollars that are sent out of this country back into countries like Mexico.

The problem here of course is because we are more divided we will be all that much weaker with the next major conflict we face as a nation. And it will come. A people have always had to resist and struggle to gain or maintain freedom for themselves or to pass it on to others. With the economic and military rise of the strong totalitarian regimes currently on this planet, and our apparent lack of resolve to stand up to them, we will have to see a major conflict of staggering proportions again in the future. If for no other reason than the Western lifestyle, based largely on self-determination, we present a threat to them by our very existence because it is diametrically opposed to their approach to governance. But this time, unlike in WWII, we will face it as a much weaker nation, and this will primarily be because we are divided along the lines of *language, law, and allegiance.*

Predatory Lending
In recent years the term *"Risked Based Lending"* has taken on a new and a more severe meaning. What it originally meant was

that lenders could extend loans based on interest rates that reflected the risk presented to loan payback based on the credit scores of the applicants. Basically this means the worse your credit, the higher your interest rate. This seemed fair at the time because individuals who at one time couldn't qualify for a decent home, car, or other big ticket items could now do so without bank examiners raising too much of an eyebrow. All the lending institution had to do was charge enough interest so that if even half the loan was repaid, they would still have gotten back at least the capital they originally extended and possibly more.

This however opened the floodgates to businesses that only a generation ago may have faced usury or loan sharking charges for the inordinate amount of interest they charge to those that are the least able to pay them back. Consumers are trapped within the grips of these super high interest loans in much the same way an addict is trapped by their dealer. They are undoubtedly called predatory because they prey on those who are most vulnerable to them. They ask the question, "Where else are you going to go?"

Predatory lending implies help for those facing financial hardships and because of their credit scores are without the normal borrowing alternatives of a bank, credit union, or reputable finance company to turn to. But in truth this practice operates in much the same fashion as do drug dealers. It promises a quick solution to a difficult problem and in the end brings about far more problems for many consumers than they ever solved.

These organizations line the streets of depressed communities. They teach and send the message that trapping and consuming a large portion of someone's household income is fine. You just have to say (or make yourself believe) that you are providing a good service and that in the end it was their decision to come to you. You are only a merchant with a product for sale; not drugs but high interest dollars. They both do the same thing though. Create a return clientele based on the weakness and eventual ruin of the customer. The challenge is then to squeeze out every drop of money from them that you can until that time comes.

Racism: Valid question or overused excuse?

Mankind has always been able to think of new and creative reasons to hate and kill his neighbor. When the people of earth were largely nomadic, the booty or possessions of other tribes were reason enough to invade and rob them. Later when we became nations, nationalism, the land or borders of other nations, became a major synergist for war. And even later, as we became "more advanced," religion became a prime motivator in the destruction and subjugation of others.

Racism though, comparatively speaking, is fairly new on the scene as a reason to hate and subjugate. While anti-Semitism and the belief that those of African nations or decent were not human predate the founding of this nation, in our times it basically stems from and was formalized in Darwinism, which put forth the first broadly accepted scientific classification of mankind by racial species, and propagated the notion of the "preservation of favored species." Adolf Hitler would later pick up on this and use it to make his point for the genocide of his fellow German and Austrian citizens who were of Jewish heritage. The problem was that Darwin didn't have the benefit of the knowledge of DNA. If he had he, would have realized that except for less than 1% of our genetic coding all humans are genetically identical.

Yet the question of racism is indeed a valid topic and one that I hope to address in depth in a future publication for its cultural and pathological dynamics. But for the sake of expediency, in this work we will investigate only a few short points as it pertains to our topic.

To illustrate this I must use practical examples. As a counselor I can tell you that people always hate this part. Seeing ourselves is

94

never easy. But when we really see ourselves and if we become uncomfortable with what is there, that really is a good thing most of the time. Because we must first become uncomfortable before we are forced to make changes. We don't even change positions in beds or our seats unless we first become uncomfortable.

Racism affects:
a) ***The Way We Relate -*** I am always amazed that with all the clear and present dangers to our nation that exist, and with American military personnel fighting and dying in several different theaters of war, that some citizens are still engaged in a struggle within their own nation that for most of us ended over 150 years ago. A struggle, which even though may not be physical, is still against fellow citizens. The Civil War regardless of your views on it should be like any past war... over. How can we look at those of middle-eastern heritage and comment on how long they remember insult or injury when many of us stand guilty of the same?

Numerous states initially fought President Reagan's signing into law the Dr. Martin Luther King Holiday. They did not seem to view it as a day to honor an American that refused to do violence, risking and eventually laying down his life so that the words of our noble constitution could be realized for *all* Americans regardless of race. How much more patriotic or American can you be as when you defend liberty and equality? But rather these states seemed to have viewed it, at least initially, as a racial issue. So in what appeared to be an act to sooth the pain of losing a battle in a war, some states passed laws for confederate holidays to counter.

One of my major concerns in this instance is that those motivations behind such actions will undoubtedly be passed down to another generation of American children who don't deserve and can't afford to inherit a house divided mentality.

b) ***The way we legislate and hire*** – The most obvious
contemporary legislation connected to race is *Affirmative
Action Legislation.* And the great divide of our times on such
legislation centers on the question of whether it does us good
or harm.

To my knowledge I have never received affirmative action
quota based employment. And to my knowledge neither have
my siblings or any of our children, those old enough to work.
I don't believe that I am the type of individual that sees a racist
behind every tree. That being said let me share with you some
of my own personal experience with race in the workplace.

Once I worked as an employment counselor for a private firm
that, among other human resource functions, performed search
or "headhunter" services for the businesses it took on as
clients. I traveled more often during this period of my life and
as a result, my accent, which is distinctly *geechy,* was not as
thick as it is now. So on the phone, most people couldn't
identify whether I was black or white. And while it didn't
happen that often, I had occasions where a client would
instruct me when I was hiring for a particular position that
they needed filling, not to hire blacks.

Affirmative Action Legislation, at least in theory, was enacted
to level the playing field because racial discrimination in the
workplace is a fact. So if you eliminate it, what do you replace
it with? Nepotism, favoritism, cronyism, and sexual
harassment also exist in the workplace, and no one is
advocating getting rid of the laws protecting us against them.
But race is a high profile and ultra sensitive issue. One reason
for that is because no one wants to be portrayed as being so
racist that it affects our honesty and integrity. But in reality, in
some of us it does. Another reason discussing race is so
difficult is because race has become overused as a catchall for
far too many perceived inequities, both societal and

vocational, when many times these perceived inequities in reality have more to do with the lack of preparedness of the individual than with the racial views of society or perspective employers.

Lastly are these laws producing their desired results? I ask this question because in my opinion the one single group that has benefited more since enactment of this legislation is white females, followed closely by black females. It has opened not only the doors of the workplace and management, but has seriously fractured the glass ceiling of corporate America. Female managers and small business owners have grown exponentially under these laws, while recruitment of African American males under these same laws often falls a distant second.

Race; faith, and orientation- A crisis of identity:

Faith and contrast – Islam is the fastest growing major religion in the world today. It is also the only known religion today where many of its prominent figures view attacks against the West as justifiable Jihad. This fact is admittedly and unavoidably a matter of national security, but it should not cast condemnation on the many peaceful and productive citizens of this country who also happen to be Muslim in their faith. It is pointed out here only to emphasize the imperative nature of the question: why is there such a strong an interest in this religion for many young African-American males? Not being an expert on religion, I will attempt to address this question based on personal experience and logic.

I believe that there is a spiritual portion to all of us, a part that longs for a connection to something or someone greater than our selves; something to give our lives, our existence meaning. Anthropologists tell us that one thing most cultures past and present share is a system and object of worship. The desire for the spiritual seems to be innate. Therefore, a major consequence of not addressing this instinctive searching is plausibly an emptiness and lack of purpose. This numbness can be manifested in a sense of hopelessness and the nagging question of, "Is this all there is?"

Why is Islam filling this void for the young African American males that convert to it? Why is the local Christian church, the faith they have in most cases been exposed to more than any other over the course of their lives, apparently not meeting their spiritual need? Consider some of the following:

1. It is becoming more and more difficult to see any contrast in lifestyle, speech, and dress codes between supposedly Christian congregational members and those of individuals who are secular and claim no religious affiliations or beliefs whatsoever. The question of many young people looking for something to believe in might be, "Why should I go to church when there is little or no difference in church members and non-church members that I can see?" Islam consistently offers a stronger contrast in all these areas. *(More on this in Chapter VI "Back into bondage; A lack of Spirituality")*

2. Islam offers worship and fellowship that does not look down on them because of their race. Predominantly white churches are still largely at a loss on how to treat black visitors or members. I have been in congregations such as this and have had people avoid sitting next to me as though I had an invisible force field around me. Either that or only another male would sit next to me. Females and young children were for the most part obviously excluded from sitting next to me and at times anywhere in my immediate vicinity. But to their credit, many are at least trying to make a transition away from segregated worship services and membership.

The greater problem lies with perception and living. Most of the blacks that I have spoken with that subscribe to Islam see Christianity as a white man's religion. They have learned doctrine or teaching that support their views and makes sense to them. So in an era when many black children are taught almost from birth to blame their problems on whites, if they are also taught at some point in life that Christianity is indeed a white man's faith, it can be very difficult to get them to follow it.

Society doesn't help in this matter. Most of the pictures that are portrayed of Jesus give him very strong European features. Movies made with biblical themes often exclude blacks except in very subservient roles, when in reality, if you look at the part of the world where most of biblical history unfolds, either of those scenarios would be almost impossible.

These young men also see more consistency among their fellow Muslims locally and worldwide in living the teachings of their faith. They see the dedication to the regimen of prayer not just taught at their local Mosques but lived out practically in their fellows. They see dress codes that are distinctive and adhered to because it is the consistently taught expectation of their faith. They see men taking prominent places in their assembly when in far too many Christian churches women outnumber men. Even in traditional two parent households when fathers elect to stay home and put the responsibility on the shoulders of mother for the church attendance of their children, male children of that household statically will opt out of all church attendance as soon as they are able to do so. *(More about this in Chapter VI "Possible Solutions)*

The hierarchy of weighted perceptions – Perceptions (the ways in which we discern or interpret our environment) in most individuals are weighted and prioritized by the level of seriousness they attribute to them. Perception can be likened to the view of *self* in Maslow's "Hierarchy of Needs" where we tend to necessarily see the fundamental and primary elements of our being such as food and shelter as much weightier matters than those say of *self-actualization.* In much the same manner, we also give weight or importance to the ambient factors of our environment. The concept *self-actualization,* though at the top or final level in the hierarchy, is much lower in priority than the weightier matters just mentioned, and is even viewed by many as an abstract concept - not a true "need" at all. Similarly, our practical views of our environment are also prioritized in the order of importance or weight we give to the factors or elements found therein. For instance, one would likely give the perception of the element of war much more weight than one might give to the perception of the newest type of computer on the market. Though both are obviously important, a war for most of us would impact our perception much more so than a computer no matter how innovative. I refer to this phenomenon as our *Hierarchy of Weighted Perceptions.*

Likewise, on our *hierarchy of weighted perceptions* most of us see race as something more concrete and fundamental than behavior. It is a given that race is seen as something indisputably physiological, while sexual orientation can be connected to behavior aside from physiology. Individuals can be of one sex physically and behave as the opposite sex without any proven physiological reason. There are also many which attest to the fact that their sexual orientations have changed, something that will never happen or be disputed with race.

When race is equated with something on a different or lower level of our hierarchy it may also be viewed with less impact or weight in our perception. When young blacks are told that their race is the equivalent of a sexual orientation or behavior what is the message and the resultant view of self? I am aware that some sexual orientations are also minority segments of our overall population. But so are physicians, manufacturing workers, and geriatric females; all these groups, by the way, feel with some validity that they have been "put upon" for various reasons. This similarity in the way groups "feel" does not justify a valid comparison or necessarily make these things the same.

In spite of this, there is routine and growing acceptance today of comfortably paralleling and putting the African American race into the same category or viewing it within the same context or connotation as sexual orientation. When it comes to blacks, many appear accepting that there is very little difference between the concepts of race and orientation. However, whites of every sexual orientation rarely if ever equate their race with anything. To them, it is so much of a given and an absolute that discussion, debate, or loose association with less-weightier perceptions are not even considerations. The result of this is that it greatly assists them racially in having a rock solid view of identity and place in the culture. It also fosters confidence and direction.

Ignorance as a commodity
The term ignorance is not used here to denote an insult but to describe a lack of knowledge or socially advancing perspective due to an insufficient level of awareness. This ignorance could be at the individual, cultural, or national level. Along this line, I have observed that there are nations, cultures, and organizations where the economic and social gap between those in power and the common citizen or rank and file is in extreme contrast. In such systems, leaders often live in comparatively luxurious surroundings providing for themselves and their families extravagantly in almost every aspect while those without the reins of power often live in poverty and want.

Now you may say that this is nothing unusual and site our own country's political process and structure as an example, because admittedly, it's very hard to get elected to public office these days unless you are independently wealthy, have a high level of contributors, or both. However, this is not the kind of situation to which I am referring. I firmly believe that even the poorest Americans fare sumptuously by most of the world's standards. For instance, many of the homeless that I have worked with over the years have been overweight... many to the point of morbid obesity. And in the end we still have a republic where voting our leaders in or out is the rule of law.

I refer to systems where there is obvious and often harmful disparity between the resources of leaders and the rank and file and where voting is not high on the list of ways that leaders are chosen. I wondered why the followers or citizenry in such systems would still be so loyal to individuals who were, in my opinion, obviously dubious concerning their own personal agendas and showing very little real concern for their plights beyond token gestures and rhetoric.

Totalitarian regimes, which depend on strong-armed or militaristic tactics against their own citizenry to enforce their will, can possibly be one but certainly not the best example of such systems. In such regimes it is painfully apparent how dissent is discouraged and muted. Yet even where there is a strong military or paramilitary enforcement presence, there must also be the realization that it is very likely made up predominantly of common citizens, illustrating that the rank and file citizenry or follower in such systems will consistently be divided into two groups. First, there are always going to be that faction who inwardly disagrees with the common or popular ideology, but the fear of being ostracized or retaliated against will keep them silent and at bay. And secondly, there will always be the blind unquestioning loyalist: those who believe with religious zeal the rhetoric of their leaders and have never questioned them on any level because of simple yet powerful indoctrination. The sad part here is that in far too many instances they are the majority. Some of the latter also undoubtedly view their own unquestioning loyalty and commitment as ways to advance and gain power.

After much observation and analysis I finally became aware of the real glue that holds such systems together in most cases. I saw what is known as the art of *slight of hand* being practiced. Magicians technically refer to it as *"misdirection."* It was being practiced with learned precision. In fact, these leaders were so good at it, unless you lived outside that particular system or alliance it was hard to catch. And if you were born into such a system where their contrivance was fed to you from birth, it was almost impossible to detect. In short, the leaders had developed a method of focusing the attention of the masses on a common perceived enemy from the outside. And they had so indoctrinated their lesser fellows that they could only focus on *the enemy without*. The problem was that *the enemy without* was not the one immediately capitalizing on their ignorance, their lack of perspective. *The enemy without* was in reality not abusing them. *The enemy without* was not faring sumptuously within their midst while they continued being economically, psychologically, socially repressed and bitter. On the contrary it was their leaders.

A friend of mine once shared something that his father had told him. He said that most times *"people don't know because they have not been taught."* While I agreed with the statement in principle, I informed him that the other side of it was that *people often resist teaching*. They do so mainly because teaching prompts learning, learning calls for change, and change demands effort. There is often immense work and emotional anguish required in the reshaping of even a portion of one's worldview. And while these two views of why ignorance prevails in so many situations were different, I thought them complimentary and not so much divergent. But here is where we shared true consensus. We both agreed that even when nations, cultures, or individuals become so disenchanted with their state of existence that they become receptive to teaching and change, their leaders, having a vested interest in their continued ignorance and mental subjugation, will surely seek to derail the process. Their reason in most cases is that the profits, gains, and adulation that they have become comfortable with would be in serious jeopardy if the views of the citizenry or rank and file changed even by the smallest of margins.

Is ignorance a commodity? I believe that it is. It has specific use, can have real monetary value, and can be transferred from person to person or generation to generation. It is a real product.

Zero Sum Restraints
The United States has an immigration problem for a reason. Just as many individuals view it as the "Land of opportunity" today as they have since our inception as a nation. We have been responsible for creating more millionaires, billionaires, entrepreneurs and inventors than any other nation in the recorded history of the world. Beginning with the Industrial Revolution and the process of "mass production," that ultimately made the commercialization of two major American inventions, the airplane and the automobile possible we begin to set the pace for the rest of the world to follow. Then with the discovery and harnessing of nuclear power as a viable source of energy and the refinement of rocket technology we left everyone else just standing in awe. We have been responsible for more space exploration than other nation on this planet. And when you consider how our cutting edge pharmaceuticals have boosted life expectancy the term "Land of Opportunity" seems to be putting it mildly.

But none of these triumphs and gains would be possible without the wonderful combination of a democratic republic style of government and a capitalist style economic system.

The role of drugs in socialization: The Social Prime Meridian
At the heart of this social decline is the launching pad for the next generation of lower echelon foodservice workers. Everything else will move out from this point of reference. Many young women

who had unwedded and early first pregnancies, if they are honest will look back and see that in some way the use of alcohol and/or other mood altering substances was involved. Just as many young men of the same ilk will look back, and if they are honest, will also admit that some mood altering substance(s) was involved in or lead up to the sexual relationship that was responsible for conceiving another human life.

The brain's inhibitory system as well as its ability to make accurate judgments is impaired with the use of many mood altering substances. Without those two basic defenses in place we tend to be open to behaviors that can carry with it sever and lasting consequences

These substances are used in spite of the body's attempt to warn us of their dangers. The reason that there is so much coughing involved with the first use of cigarettes is that because the body is protecting itself by rejecting toxins. The continued use of nicotine trains the body how to suffer an addictive toxin for the sake of its mood altering affects. Once properly trained to use one mood altering toxin the mind and the body can then tolerate another level of consumption and stimulation. Not only is the use of the original toxin likely to increase, but the gateway has been opened for the future use of more potent toxins which provide more potent stimulation and sensations. Everyone that uses nicotine doesn't go on to use controlled substances. But as a formerly certified addictions counselor I have never seen any addict in the final, most serious stage of their addiction, who had not utilized nicotine and cannabis, in that order, at the onset of their drug use.

Alcohol, a legal drug, is said to be a *"social lubricant."* It is described this way because it is used by many in social settings to "loosen up and relax." This happens with alcohol use because it affects judgment and inhibitions, our normal moral and mental safeguards. It is also often at the core of the debate for the legalization of other drugs. Proponents believe that most drugs can be used socially or recreationally much in the same manner as alcohol, and that their users should be afforded the same rights and held to the same level of responsibility as users of alcohol.

I mention the legalization argument here only to demonstrate the rationalization of many for the use of currently illegal drugs. This is also one of the more popular arguments or methods used to induce new users of illicit substances by those who have a vested interest in their lack of judgment and inhibition.

Drugs sales are often a means for financial independence for many young African American males. Those who choose to do this for the quick comparatively large sums of money they can acquire are willing to take the risks involved in possible incarceration, turf wars, and possible addiction to the substance themselves. They do so because 1.) This form of gaining money is considered a viable means of support in their clique or subculture; 2.) It fits into the short-term reward system mentality of their clique or subculture; 3.) It is often considered glamorous by females of their clique or subculture; 4.) Large sums of cash and material possessions are often equated to security and can make gaining the female that he desires to have a sexual relationship with that much easier to access.

The Prime Meridian slices through the center of the earth like a knife, and except in Greenwich England where it originates, it is invisible. Yet it begins the countdown for every hour of the earth's rotation on its axis. Everything that happens across this globe is touched and influenced by a line that you can't even see, except at its point of origin. But it is there.

In much the same way, the use of mood altering substances in adolescent interpersonal relationships becomes the Social Prime Meridian for far too many African American youths, youths that have limited or no accountability to the kind of family structure that is likely to teach and model responsible socialization. Consequently, their first serious relationship, which directly or indirectly involves these substances, is often marred by the sexually promiscuous behavior that will almost certainly culminate in a significantly increased risk of pregnancy and/or disease. The fallout from both can and often do set the social, vocational, and economic tempo for the rest of their lives and the lives of their offspring.

CHAPTER IV

CRIMINAL INTENT

One of the main reasons offered me as a counselor explaining why so many African American males (especially in, but not limited to, the Southeast) remain working in the lower paid positions of the Foodservice/Fast Food Industry, is the possession of a prior criminal record. Former clients and others have told me repeatedly that they were not given the opportunity in the job market to enter higher paid levels of employment because of the background check requirements of for many of those positions. I am told that in many cases that having any criminal record at all, felony or misdemeanor will automatically eliminate them from consideration for employment in most industries. Foodservice seems to be one of the few industries that will allow them to make at least minimal living subsistence, and for most individuals with prior convictions this is probably true. Criminal convictions can eliminate someone from a variety of different careers. And while there are many times legitimate concerns about risk, security, and underwriting associated with some criminal convictions, bias and stigma alone toward individuals with a prior criminal history can also present a devastating barrier to meaningful employment. Meaningful employment as used here is defined as employment that will allow an individual or a household to live above the poverty line.

While it may be easy for some of us to say; *"This is the price you pay for violating the law,"* this statement, though true, is not free of its downside when it is the mantra heard by a generation of young men newly released from incarceration. And here is why: 1) there is an industry of both commercial advertising and music entertainment preaching 24-7 that you are nothing without material possessions and it is reinforced in the greater society; 2) You have several generations that have been indoctrinated to this thinking, each more thoroughly and intensely than the last; and 3), you have a culture that advances the systematic view of *survival of the fittest* to explain our current rein as the ruling species on the planet.

Without a doubt there should be consequence involved in the breaking of rules, familial or societal. Coexistent with this should be a societal response to a problem that has and will continue to affect us all more and more. And remember, building more prisons maybe one part of the solution, but please keep in mind that prisons are a response to things that have already happened. Someone once said *"An ounce of prevention is worth a pound of cure."*

I will not take the high road here. Rather I will share with you some of my own personal biases on this matter and why I possess them. You may be able to relate.

In the past most time that I've commented or spoken out on the large number of African American males in the Foodservice industry I've been met rather harshly with the statement, ***"Well at least they aren't dealing drugs."*** I am not sure the assumption that some aren't selling drugs is a logical or practical one. I will explain why. But even before I give you my explanation or reasoning, I'd like to ask the question, *are they the only choices… foodservice or drugs dealing? Isn't there a stopping place somewhere in between these points?*

Criminal thinking
What is *criminal thinking*? Well according to one theory, which I believe carries substantial weight and evidence, individuals approach life with two basic perspectives of thought: *responsible or criminal thinking*. It also states that we are all on a continuum between these two extremes, which is to say that we have the ability to progress or digress in either direction between the two. We can move all the way from being ***totally responsible*** to being ***extremely criminal*** based solely on our choices. And while we are constantly afforded the opportunity for change in either direction

109

through these daily choices that we make, at a point in time which is different for everyone, we become comfortable with the way we have chosen to negotiate life, our placement on the continuum. And in the absence of outside intervention, we will remain relatively fixed at this point.

The actual continuum itself is divided into 4 segments. In between the two extreme categories we mentioned are also two more very interesting categories that further highlight or explain the progression away from responsibility and towards criminality as a mentality and way of life. They are the ***non-arrestable irresponsible*** and ***arrestable-irresponsible*** categories.

So we begin with the ***totally responsible*** individual who accepts full responsibility for their behavior regardless of the environment or circumstances they find themselves in.
Next, there is the ***non-arrestable irresponsible*** individual who will accept responsibility most of the time for their behavior but will make excuses. The things that they are irresponsible in are not matters for which one can normally be arrested. For instance, this individual may be late paying bills and will blame everyone but himself. While paying your bills late is very irresponsible, we don't have debtors prison in our society, so in most cases this is not an arrestible offense.

However, when we progress to the next phase, ***arrestible irresponsible***, we find that this individual will accept responsibility for their behavior only if they are caught in the act or discovered after the fact, and will still seek to make excuses. They possess some of the same attributes of the ***extreme criminal*** thinker but to lesser degrees. They are self centered, dubious, secretive, and subscribes easily to risky behavior with little regard for rules or laws.

The last phase on the continuum is the ***extreme criminal*** thinker. This is someone who will never accept responsibility for his or her behavior under any circumstance. Even if he is caught on camera, he will likely deny that the individual on the screen is truly him. At this point the criminal act is less important than the thinking. For the same thinking that will allow for the stealing of five dollars from a mother or grandmother's purse without conscience is the same thinking that will allow for the killing of that parent or grandparent without conscience. In their mind neither act is the fault of the *extreme criminal* thinker since they never accept responsibility for their behavior.

The main concept that should not go unnoticed here is that at some point along the continuum the individual becomes so irresponsible in their behavior that they begin to commit acts for which they can be arrested, adjudicated, and incarcerated. While incarceration is necessary when applied solely by itself, it is often not an effective intervention for criminal thinking. This is because the criminal thinker is basically thrown into a pool of other criminal thinkers for the length of his or her incarceration. There he or she will likely and logically become a "better" criminal thinker. And then they are eventually released.

However, with proper intervention, incarceration can be an opportune time for professionals, trained in criminal thinking and forensics counseling, to address and solicit change in the criminal thought processes of the individual. I have actually seen a cognitive behavioral approach utilized as the basis of a phased therapeutic forensic clinical program that actually assisted probationer clients in moving away from the criminal extreme to the totally responsible end of the continuum with lasting change. I worked in such a pilot program for approximately three years that had a stunning observable, success rate that was repeatable, and sustainable. It worked well, that is, until politics destroyed it.

Politician and clinician are different jobs and should never be confused, and in defense of clinicians, I don't know many of them wish to be politicians. But politicians often hold the appropriations purse stings especially for public institutions. Many politicians seem to really want to do a good job, so I believe it would do well if they worked more with the input of direct service clinicians and/or first line supervision. This would better insure a more effective approach to the use of limited public funds for what is ultimately the protection of the individual citizens who elected them.

Incarceration also provides a propitious time for religious or spiritual interventions that have also produced observable and permanent changes in the thought process and lifestyle of the convert. The only caveat here obviously is the problem that arises when the incarcerated individual becomes a proselyte of a religious doctrine that espouses or promotes violence against others. And then they are released.

Without intervention and upon release it almost guarantees that we have someone whose basic thinking and approach to life has not changed. Foodservice work is one of the quickest ways of meeting the need for immediate income or the basic work requirement of those on any form of supervised released, but here's the problem. In much the same way that you will infect a healthy group of individuals by exposing them to someone with cold or other transmittable physical maladies, you stand a very good chance of infecting the thought and behavioral processes of healthy individuals by exposing them to criminal thinkers. If this were not true, why would responsible parents care about who their children associate with?

Parentally speaking, when our son was of age and wanted to begin working at first I discouraged him from looking for work in Fast Food. My reason being that because of my job, I knew that there could possibly be a number of other young African American males he might be exposed to that had a history of prior violent and/or drug related felonies. But more than that, I also believed from experience that most of them would probably still possess uncorrected criminal thinking and intent. Not all my reasons or my beliefs stemmed only from professional experience however, but was grounded in logical deduction connected to the statement made by those who were offended at my even mentioning this phenomena; i.e. ***"Well at least they aren't dealing drugs."***

Logical Deduction #1: It is extremely difficult to afford the aesthetic accoutrements such as the jewelry, video and music systems, expensive cell phones, and automobile accessories that most adolescent and young adults desire today on a Fast Food salary alone. So where will those funds come from if you live in a single parent home that has income below or close to the poverty level? There are only two legal choices evident to me. They are either the sacrifice of single mothers to provide those things, or those same young men working two jobs. And according to the U.S. Department of Labor the young African American male is not the profile of the average individual who works two jobs.

Logical Deduction # 2: It has been my experience as a counselor working in both employment and forensics that the average profile of the young African American male (18-34) employed in foodservices is very similar to the average profile of the young African American male in the criminal justice system. Most I have worked with have been from single parent households (mother with no father present), have had relatively low academic scores, and multiple criminal offenses at the adult and/or juvenile level. This stands to reason, as foodservice is one of the surest vocational placements for inmates upon release from incarceration, and significant portions of these individuals were originally incarcerated for drug related offenses and will very often re-offend upon release.

****

The almost continuous array of young African American males across the nightly news arrested or wanted for violent and drug related offenses ought to cause everyone major concern. Yet society seems virtually silent as the situation only worsens. Whites are afraid of sounding prejudice, and blacks are concerned with not airing our dirty laundry in public. Rest assured, that ship has sailed.

So let me say to blacks and whites: Political correctness may have its merits, but I have yet to see them. Political correctness only helps us to walk around the elephant in the room. It neither alleviates the elephant nor the obvious problems associated with keeping it in ones living room.

My son eventually took a job in Fast Food anyway. His mom and I both agreed to it because it was a well-known Christian owned chain where many of his friends were employed and he didn't have to work on Sundays. He is in college today with a part time job in retail. But when he comes home on breaks he is still able to pick hours on the schedule of that restaurant if he wishes. Were my concerns valid? I think so.

Young people need to be taught within the confines of the family structure that the more irresponsible they are, the more freedoms they lose. They must also be taught within the same environment that the farther they progress into the irresponsible/criminal lifestyle the, fewer alternatives they will possess. In our society once we have proven we can't be trusted with our choices, someone else will choose for us.

The role of drugs in crime: Chasing The Dragon (The Story of Me)

"Chasing the dragon" is a drug term with biblical implications to say the least. I believe it is significant to heroine use and encompasses the total experience of seeking, using, and the high gained from the substance. I use it here to allude to the experience of the first high acquired from most mood altering substances. That particular experience is usually so phenomenal and intense that the user can and often will seek for a lifetime to experience it once

more. They can never recapture it, but no addict in active addiction can ever be convinced of this. All of their usage from that point on is spurred by the hunt or chase for the ever-elusive level of stimulation of that first encounter. An experience usually so new and intense that all other life factors seem to cease to exist for the moment, and in their place only the extreme euphoria of the new drug.

I know there are many that kick against the idea of genetic predisposition when it comes to addictions. But I assure you that most of them have never had a dependence problem of any consequence. I will also not argue the physiological and psychopharmacological aspects of addiction in this work. Though profound and significant, I will convey my own experiences with addiction from a personal perspective.

****

I was born in the mid-fifties and did most of my real growing up in the late sixties and early seventies. My parents were married but separated and my father, a naval Korean War vet, died when I was a very young boy. I am the eldest of five siblings, and most of my life that I can recall was spent in a single parent household similar in some ways to the ones of which I write about in this book. Most of my childhood experiences are from a rural or suburban environment but many are from a purely urban environment as I lived in both. Looking back, I can see much dysfunction in our family social unit. But through all of it, my mother had some basic staples that were nonnegotiable. They were education, manners, clean clothing (no matter the age), and church. These elements of my formative years would not keep me from making mistakes in life. However, I believe they were and are essential and fundamental to my continuing recovery from those mistakes.

My childhood was not easy. Because I was the eldest child and had no father or older brother around, I was on my own for most of my school and boyhood experiences. The term "kids can be cruel" in my case was an understatement. I was considered a nerd (bookworm was the expression back then). I was not as strong or athletic as other boys my age was, not acquiring my full muscular development and strength until much later in adolescence. But I was still usually always taller than most kids, making me an easy target for bullies trying to make a name for themselves for whatever reasons or insecurities that drives bullies.

If you were not athletic as a child in the era I grew up in, the label "no good" would be attached to you. This is a tremendously defeating stigma for a fatherless child to wear daily around their neck. And if you have the misfortunate combination of being bright but not strong or attractive and no father or older siblings around to protect you, the jealousy and ire of those who are not as intellectually gifted are free to act in reprisal with little fear of impunity. I was often said to be "acting white" by other children (especially in my urban school experience) because for most of my schooling I received good grades. This was a requirement of my mother. But because of this, I experienced beatings at the hands of individuals who have long since forgotten the blood they drew, the swellings they imposed and the sheer dread they instilled in me of just getting up and facing another day in a school system that seemed to care as little for me as I eventually came to care for it.

In those turbulent times of tremendous social upheaval in which I grew up, drugs were (for the most part) idealized and many were considered socially acceptable. The use of many drugs was also considered as indications of enlightenment and even spirituality. I had experienced a few of them. But marijuana augmented by some form of alcohol was the combination that I chose most often. This was also true for the group that I normally socialized with. Some only drank alcohol and some only used marijuana. But most of us used the aforementioned combination with marijuana receiving the heaviest usage. I have never knowingly done heroine and for many years refused several offers of cocaine until ultimately and

116

regrettably giving in. For some reason I feared those two substances above all others. I had seen what heroine use had done to many individuals and was not impressed. And while cocaine was at the time highly glamorized and purported by many to be only psychologically addicting, it did not alleviate the intrinsic and eerie discomfort I used to receive from just seeing the drug.

I still recall the day that I returned to using marijuana. It was a long holiday weekend. The gang had gotten together to go to the beach. My wife would not come with us. Admittedly she did not enjoy the water near as much as I did because she was not a swimmer. Still it angered me when she refused to go with us because I really desired she and my daughter to be with me. But this was something that she had been doing more and more lately. Leaving me to make excuses and feel awkward over her obvious absences at social events. I had discharged from the military so that we would not be separated and now, in my young mind at least, she was thumbing her nose at what I saw as a sacrifice on my behalf for the purpose of making my family stronger. I just couldn't understand what seemed to me as her abandonment. Many things, I'd learn after our breakup, were happening inside her mind also. But I was blind to them back then.

Another thing that angered and hurt me was that my friends were the same individuals that the both of us socialized with before and after we were married. It was only after we became committed to our faith that our circles of friends changed. So I had gone backwards so to speak, and she undoubtedly saw this. At the time, all I wanted to believe was that she was being snobbish (which she could actually be at times) Looking back though, I no longer believe that was the case in this particular instance.

At the beach when one of my cousins offered me the chance to smoke a joint of "new stuff" with him, I did it more in vengeance than anything else. It would take a while for my use to return to and surpass its old levels. But it would. For a while I was fine with just sneaking off to my workshop and smoking in there on Saturday mornings when my wife and daughter were usually off shopping. That would change also.

There is a New Testament scripture (Luke 11:24-26 KJV) that says: *When the unclean spirit is gone out of a man, he* (the unclean spirit) *walketh through dry places, seeking rest; and finding none, he saith, I will return unto my house whence I came out. And when he cometh, he findeth it swept and garnished. Then goeth he, and taketh to himself seven other spirits more wicked than himself; and they enter in, and dwell there: and the last state of that man is worse than the first.* In addictions therapy this can be equated with the phenomena known as "progression." It is the belief that the disease of addiction progresses in the psyche of the addict minus overt symptoms even when they quit using. However if they choose to pick up again, in a relatively short period of time they will be using at or above their previous levels and their lives will be in the same or worse disarray. I witnessed this fact in myself and would see it replayed in others many times over.

And so our problems became more complicated by not only the fact that we had ceased to communicate with each other, but that we also had begun to socialize in different circles. But the real meltdown wouldn't occur until I left my old company for a much better paying job. Suddenly I was making more money than I had in my lifetime. I also moved into some very influential positions over many individuals. And I was still in my mid-twenties.

My circle of so called friends increased. My hours of work and socializing got to be later and later. And by this time my wife had ceased to attend anything with me, even church services. Usually it would be just my daughter and I. I am certain she had stopped believing in me.

Now back to my point concerning predisposition. One night I gave in and I tried cocaine with several other individuals. At some point

118

during the night all those individuals, including the person that introduced me to the substance, left and went their way to get some rest so that they could meet their obligations of the coming day; all of them that is except for me. This would not be the last time unfortunately that my bent or predisposition for this substance in particular would show itself to my detriment.

A number of years later after I had been in a program of recovery for eighteen months I went out to celebrate the completion of an engineering project with several other professionals. When I was hospitalized in treatment 1 ½ years earlier just prior to discharge a nurse had warned me that even though alcohol was not my drug of choice, none the less as an addict, if I used it, it could possibly lead me back to my drug of choice. On the night in question everyone left the restaurant/bar that we had gone to for our celebration prior to closing; everyone that is except me. I went looking for cocaine and did not show up again on my job for another three days. Needless to say, for many reasons I believe in predisposition on both physical and metaphysical or spiritual levels.

Cocaine on the street has many names; "girl, white girl, snow, blow" etc. Interestingly enough some I have known have called it the "Devil on Earth." In the bible the Devil has many names; "Satan, the Enemy, Lucifer" et al. In Genesis he is know as "The Serpent." However in Revelation he is known as "the Dragon." And I chased it for approximately seven years from the point of where I first picked it up and eventually put it down.

In those seven years I became involved in white-collar crime, stealing the money that I needed to support my addiction. I lived a life of lies and shadows. I walked in the places of the dead. I saw the hopeless and brought them nothing but desolation. I lived the life of a criminal and an addict. I lost my family, my property, my status, my job, and in due course my freedom.

Eventually, one faithful night on what I would later come to find out was my parents wedding anniversary, God opened my eyes to the truth I needed to see. He showed me that drugs and alcohol were really two big bullies that I was fighting. The only problem was that they were so strong and so smart that I could never defeat them. Which begged the question, why continue the fight? So that night I gave up. I resolved that I would not walk down the street on the way home where I knew they waited. I would not flirt any longer with the idea that maybe today I could beat them. All the evidence was against this notion. And besides, they had taken almost everything from me but my life. It was all that was left, and I am sure they wanted it as well. So I resolved that if these bullies, these tyrants didn't come looking for me I would listen to whoever I needed to listen to, work any step, close my mouth, and learn any rule in order to keep from going out searching for them.

That night I slept in my car outside what would be my last treatment center until daybreak when they would have a bed after morning discharges. In that vehicle all night was a 5th of cheap vodka. I kept it hidden under the seat and out of my sight so as not to tempt myself but would still be there in case I chickened out. In that vehicle that night devoid of family, home, and self-respect, I found the seed of my faith again. I had never stopped praying for God to deliver me. But that night, when I knew I had made my decision, I once again found His warmth, strength, and comfort. I am not trying to convert anyone. But I am saying what an integral part of my recovery faith played for me.

At daybreak I took the vodka from under the seat, got out of my car, put it in the trash can outside the treatment center far under the rest of the trash so that it couldn't be found and used by others as I now saw it as poison. And I walked inside.

I spent 5 weeks hospitalized. One week of which was in the detoxification unit and another month in daily therapy. The chief therapist on my team was a Clinical Psychologist that was so well versed at her profession she inspired me to make a serious career change and become a counselor. By choice, I worked in addiction for many years at every level: direct services, first line supervisor, and administrator before attending graduate school. After which my focus was on the assisting of patients and clients to recover from trauma and life situations that is prohibitive to them gaining or returning to employment that will be something they enjoy, also give them a living wage.

Some of my best times in my current profession have been in the area of vocational job development. This is not the process of job hunting, but it is often the process of going to a business where no current vacancy is advertised and showing an employer where you can improve their operation and or save them money. Of course the positions that are developed as a result of this operations improvement will go directly to patients on your caseload.

It is in this context of a vocational rehabilitation counselor that I first began to pragmatically observe the fast food phenomena written about in this book. I had long before been emotional about it. But now I was able to balance some of that emotion with the perspective of a professional specializing in the world of work and readjustment.

As I write this, less than 3 days ago two young black females, part of the crew set to open a local fast food chain restaurant, were found dead inside after the restaurant failed to open and was reported to the police. I have been in that particular restaurant several times. It is not that far from my home, and I live on a quiet street in a middleclass residential neighborhood. They found the killer yesterday. He was also a member of that same morning crew. He reportedly shot the two women, his co-workers, after robbing them of $100.00. It was also reported that they found him hiding in a back room at his girlfriend's, and that he still had the cash and the murder weapon in his possession.

Early in my counseling career when I worked in forensics, I learned the alarming statistics of how many individuals were under the influence of some mood altering substance at the time they committed the crime for which they had been convicted and incarcerated. This in no way alleviates personal responsibility. It does however underscore the need for a direct assault by those who still care on the forces in the lives of our young people that glorify and glamorize drug and alcohol use and the materialism that is part and parcel of the quick profits of drug sales.

So, this is but a brief summary of a major aspect of my life. Because I suppose that if all the wrongful mistakes I've made were actually written, *"the world itself could not contain the books."*

Along For The Ride
I call to everyone in search of joy
To all that desire peace today
There is a journey worthy to view
I am hope, come ride I say

I have onboard as honored guests
The stars of heaven and underlings
The weak, the mighty, none turned away
From dregs to warrior kings

My promises are sure, believe me
I deliver on each to everyone
There are no favorites in my heart
My gifts are to all that ride or run

I am that white girl from off the block
I am the snow of winters present and past
The stuff and weaver of dreams, my friend
The mold, the dye, the cast

You've never seen the heights I soar
All others walk a draggled pace
In comparison to my altitude, my speed
No other loves or idols do race

But as I make each final approach
I caution all on the landings
Rougher for some than others
But for all most damning, most demanding

You see - I am that white girl from off the block
Those from streets and palaces lament
Yet as I beckon they rejoinder clear
To sweet journeys of height and brutal descent

My prices are most modest to begin, enjoy
The higher costs are farther along the way
The payment balloons at journey's end
But mind you, it's due in full that day

I'll have my merchants, just as my buyers
It's only a matter of time you see
I am that white girl from off the block
Please come and ride with me

E. Middleton

Chapter V
Nocturnal Combustion
(Burning Up the Night)

Visit any busy street or business in the nation after midnight in areas where African Americans number a significant portion of the local population. There is an extremely high chance that you will find that African Americans, especially those 34 and under, are either in the majority of those present, or at least have a disproportionately high representation in comparison with the total population demographics or breakdown of the area.

Should this matter to any of us as citizens and taxpayers? Should it matter to those of us that are African American? I believe that it matters significantly. Asking the questions of why this is and what are the causes and affects is not racist but merely taking a serious and needed look at a phenomenon that in one way or another impact us all negatively.

It is a fact that most of the nation trains, works, advances, and achieves in the workplace and that the workplace for the majority of us happens in the day. So then the question of how ready we are for that world becomes an extremely important one, especially if our social patterns are of those that I identify as *deep nocturnal* types.

I define the term "deep nocturnal socialization patterns" in brief as; repeated or sustained patterns of socialization that take place post 12:00am to near sunrise.

There are certainly many implications involved in the examination of a subject such as this. Some of those implications speak to emotional issues, others to economics. It is the matter of economic implications that we will investigate here. Though, for the sake of this discussion I believe that they are quite possibly one and the same. Allow me to explain.

Some members of the clergy that I know and have a deep regard for their teachings have a penchant for saying, "show me your checkbook, and I will show you where your heart (emotions) lies." Since one of the major signs of success in a capitalist society is the gaining of its best tool, capital, both on a personal and cultural level. Conversely the lack of that success to any notable degree often puts a person or a culture in the position of not possessing that tool but having to borrow it whenever it is needed in any significant situation, often at exorbitant rates. *(See predatory lending)*

So what are the economics involved here? Where does the capital go? What are the major consumable goods and services that attract the capitol and reap the rewards of these *deep hours dollars?* Do any of these dollars ever return to the segment from which they were assimilated? And if we continue on the premise that the average age of these spenders are between the ages of 18-34 with *deep nocturnal socialization patterns*, it might also serve well to consider how they fare in workforce-related indicators such as maximum wage earning ability, longevity, advancement, attendance, and of course performance. All of these factors obviously contribute greatly to or are actual elements of a worker's individual evaluation and reflects their value to their employer. Of course the stipulation here is that there are certainly factors other than adverse socialization patterns that can and do influence all these categories, but it should be common sense that workplace readiness and adequate sleep are directly proportional. This truth is undisputed by most responsible workers.

It seems obvious that if we wish to see where these dollars are mainly spent, the easiest way to do this would be to identify some of the major outlets for them at that time of the morning. So what are the businesses that flourish after 12am? No exhaustive studies are needed here. Visit any sizably populated town or city in the nation and you will see those convenience stores, 24-hour department stores, some fast food drive through windows, night clubs, and the sex industry which can present itself in the form of adult books and video stores and exotic dance clubs. Those are the legal operations. On the illegal side you can have prostitution, controlled substances, and gambling in prohibited states or forms.

These patterns also present implications in the criminal justice arena. Out of all African Americans incarcerated, many of them committed their crimes during those hours when most Americans are asleep. It has also been my experience that many career and first time criminal offenders frequently socialize in these hours.

It is a very easy thing in this era of extreme political correctness to blame someone else for our personal failures or the destructive acts that we may commit on self or others. There are many easily accessed excuses for us when the realization that we are cutting off our nose to spite our face becomes too painful to accept. The idea that one might be his or her own worst enemy has always been an unpopular one. It can be even more unpopular when that suggestion strikes at the heart of a group or at cultural pride, but one undeniable truth of living is that very often this is exactly the case. Many times we are indeed our own worst enemies, and whenever we fail to confront the denial of how our own behavior is harming us, the bleeding continues.

Anyone who teaches problem solving techniques will tell you that the first step is to properly identify the problem. A failure in this primary phase will ultimately lead to a solution that doesn't properly or lastingly address the problem. As a therapist I can say without reservation that denial is the most often used defense mechanism against acceptance of ones pathology or disability. It is also one of the major blockades to healing and recovery processes. and understandably so. Denial is the ultimate analgesic for the human psyche. It numbs the pain emanating from a distressful condition or event. In that way, at least initially, it can usefully assist in the acute phase of trauma. The problem is of course that denial does nothing to halt the progression of diseases or sufficiently address debilitating conditions. So when continued into what should be the post acute recovery and readjustment period, it then becomes a barrier to healing.

Whenever a condition, mentality, or mindset becomes a significant barrier or blockade in the recovery of an individual or culture, that mindset is self-destructive and therefore by its very nature pathological or sick. And, like any pathological condition left to its own device, it will often cause severe and lasting problems. At times in an individual, those problems spread from the area of the body or personality from which it originated to affect and/or infect other portions of its host. So too a pathological condition in a culture can manifest itself in areas other than the one from which it originated or was first identified in. Adverse patterns of socialization can produce adverse patterns in the area of the workplace and other areas of life.

America is a work-based society. People come to these shores from all over the world because it is widely the case that anyone who works hard here can achieve their dreams or goals. It is also one way by which we derive our status of individuality. We are strongly identified by what we do, where and how often we do it. The question then becomes, how can a generation or a culture make the best of life in a work-based society when it meets all or most workdays inadequately prepared for them?

******

The *sleep cycle* replenishes and readies humans for the next day or the next *waking cycle*. Even some of our internal constructs are based naturally on a 24-hour day. And while there are studies that suggest that brain activity also increases during periods of depravation (just as it does in periods of sleep), we are not addressing depravation that occurs during work or other productive tasks such as studying. But we are examining what happens the next day in the workforce, and we are attempting to investigate the implications to individuals and groups entering that workday deprived of the natural cycle of sleep and rest.

Deep Nocturnal Patterns; How and Why They Originated: "… **And man preferred darkness to the light…**" Some may recognize this quote as an excerpt from the book of John in the New Testament. And while this is not a religious treatise, there seems to be an enormous amount of applicability here for our topic of post 12am socialization patterns. What are the elements involved in the type of interaction that occurs prior to this time as opposed to those that occur near or after it that attracts those that it does? Is this pattern a product of environment, choice, necessity, or cultural evolution?

As stated earlier, most of tend to agree that the primary factor or building block of society is the nucleus or family social unit. Moral and spiritual principles, absolutes, work ethics, study habits, manners, prejudices, likes and dislikes for most of us can be connected to our families of origin (the family social unit we were born into). These family units need not have the traditional make up that we are accustomed to, but just provide its members with some or all of the basic functions such as identity, connection, security, and acceptance. Also as previously stated, most of the individuals that I have observed in businesses and in traffic at these hours have been African Americans. And most of them are young,. I estimate between the general ages of 14-34.

I recall vividly being in that age group and socializing in those hours and can say unequivocally that I never found anything truly good or lasting out there in those hours. Some may say that I grew out of it. That might be true. But chronology aside and on a personal note, I had my scares. It was during these hours when I was first exposed to and became addicted to mood altering substances. It was during these hours when I formed social bonds with individuals who viewed sex, honesty, relationships and other serious topics differently than what I knew to be right. And when I say "right," I am referring to standards that are generally accepted by those in the greater society, standards that do no harm to others and produce positive regard in the majority our fellow citizens.

The mindsets: We must realize that individuals who regularly keep and socialize in these deep nocturnal hours can be classified primarily in two groups or mindsets; **Hunters** and **Searchers**. All *hunters* are not males but they are predominantly so. All *searchers* are not female but they are predominantly so.

Hunters initiate from a predatory perspective. They are seeking to take advantage of others in the form of obtaining their personal property or taking pseudo-consensual advantage from a sexual standpoint. The term pseudo-consensual is used here because even though the majority of sexual liaisons that we are referencing will on the surface be viewed as consensual, I am convinced that most will be entered into under false pretenses where hunters are offering something on which they will ultimately default, mainly a long term and caring relationship. These deep nocturnal hours make both these goals more easily attained because the ambient safeguards that are present in earlier hours are now absent. We will specifically address those safeguards in the following paragraphs.

Hunters primarily have two goals, crime and/or sex. Criminally motivated hunters will usually restrict their socialization to other criminally motivated hunters during these hours. They may choose the private dwelling of one of their group. Or in the case of gangs, the meeting place may be some type of community property headquarters. Even if they chose to socialize in more obvious surroundings among others not in their group, they will normally be reclusive from the main body restricting to great degree for instance who sits at their table in a nightclub setting. In the case of hunters who have crime as their motivating factor, you have the obvious absence of daylight, which speaks to lower visibility. You also have the absence of people in greater numbers, which speaks to a lesser degree of recognition and easy identification. Both of these factors are huge deterrents for many crimes. Conversely, their absence or reduction to the criminal mindset is almost an open invitation.

In the case of hunters who have sex as their motivating factor, there is also the absence of daylight along with our usual psychological safeguards. Be it because of work, stigma, conscience, convenience, romantic affect, or our remaining modesty, as a culture we still resign much of our sexual activity to nighttime hours.

Much of the socialization in the deep nocturnal time frame can be connected, but not limited to, a nightclub setting. Individuals often utilize mood-altering substances with much more ease in this kind of atmosphere because of the high levels of social acceptance among fellow patrons and participant of the activity. There is a general expectation that most individuals present will be okay with the social use of these substances. Some teetotalers may be present but not many by comparison. With the readily available and steady flow of alcohol (and possibly other substances), the primary and protective safeguards of judgment and inhibition are diminished, and behavior becomes far more risky.

There is an ethnic cultural belief among many African American club goers that should be noted here. It is the widely held belief that the real entertainment and most meaningful social interaction usually will not take place prior to 11pm or later. So arriving earlier would be pointless and a waste of money. To overcome this dead time in their establishments, club owners often promote specials involving free or cheap alcohol to induce patrons to arrive at their establishments earlier. This is known in marketing as the *loss liter* approach or strategy. The money that they lose on individual drinks they see themselves making it back and more on the sheer volume of alcohol sold by the end off the night added to any applicable cover charges.

Some clubs will hold promotions where only females are allow in for the first hour or two of operations. They will also provide alcohol free of charge or at a greatly reduced rate during this time. After the imposed time limit they will then allow in male patrons. This has the affect and logical conclusion of making each sex more eager to interact with the other, and of softening up or breaking down the inhibitions and resistance of females to the sexual advances of males. To the hunter it is basically a social trap.

The other social type, *Searchers*, are usually motivated by loneliness and/or insecurity. These are not exclusive emotional states but common to all humans at one time or another. What's different here is how and when these conditions are addressed on average in the greater society, as opposed to how they are addressed by those of *deep nocturnal socialization patterns.*

Please do not take these emotional conditions of loneliness and insecurity lightly. I believe that they could in fact be the common threads of our society and world today. Here is why. Though all of us experience or suffer them to some degree at various intervals in our lives, what is most astounding to me as a counselor is the frequency at which I am now seeing these emotional states manifested as co-morbid or precipitating factors in acute pathological conditions both physical and psychological. In fact they have become so prominent and pronounced that they appear to be driving more and more individuals toward risky behavior to solve these emotional dilemmas.

I am convinced that loneliness and insecurity have been the biggest factors in the rise in popularity of online dating services and chat rooms. Unlike many, I do not agree that security has been the real genesis behind this trend because I see very little evidence in my opinion that these services have improved security for their users. Not if you can believe some of the network documentaries focusing on the tragedies involved in the real world culmination of many of these relationships. And online relationships are getting so common that almost everyone has at least one friend with a cyber dating horror story.

In order to address these feelings healthily, some still utilize such remedies as church and secular single groups, singles only apartment complexes, setups by friends and family members, journal writing, hobbies, talking to a counselor or members of the clergy, volunteerism, pets, shopping etc. These remedies however tend to keep one on normal (societal average) time patterns of socialization. But we are currently looking at the abnormal, so we must move on.

So what characterizes the deep nocturnal searcher? The two commonalities among most searchers are **1) They are all searching for someone, and 2) They all seem to have a fantasy ideal mate in mind** that is usually unattainable, especially in the environment in which they are seeking him or her. The image that many are usually seeking is an image from mass communications mediums such as television or celebrity magazines. But it should be obvious too most females that any males they meet at those hours will likely fall into one of three categories vocationally. 1) **They will just be getting off work from an evening shift, or 2) they will have no employmen**t or no meaningful employment that addresses long-term goals, or 3) they will not be performing well at the jobs that they do have.

Having personally worked 2nd shift employment for long periods of time, it has been my experience that not many responsible individuals will leave work at that time of night and head for a nightclub. The ones who do will probably choose to do so on a weekend night. So, 2nd shift workers are probably the smallest numbers of the three groups.

So warning signs aside, if the male meets or comes close to the fantasy image he will likely be given access. In other words, if he is attractive enough physically and/or converses well (possessing adequate humor with feigned or true empathy), and his attire and demeanor are within fad established parameters, females are far more likely to ignore the obvious and pursue a relationship with their fantasy soul mate.

But probably the thing that drives *deep nocturnal socialization patterns* more than anything else is the lack of fathers to enforce curfews in the formative years of these individuals. And not just enforcing it by the establishment of a particular time to be in bed and later in adolescence, a particular time to be back in from socializing with friends. But when working fathers are in the home, they are often the last ones in bed and regularly perform many tasks such as checking locks, lighting, and alarms to ensure the safety of the domicile and the family. This "shutting down" process also frequently includes assuring that all family members are usually settled in for the night and movement throughout the home is minimal to none. He also has the ability to set the example that the right amount of rest must be obtained to face the upcoming day at your best.

I am not saying that strong mothers cannot perform these same functions and provide the same examples. What I am saying is that it should be obvious to all of us at this point that this is not the best case scenario and is not working for the majority of children born into an absentee father environment.

Chapter VI
Back Into Bondage
(The Summation)

Chains were an anathema to slaves and their all their children that were born shortly after the Civil War. It is my opinion that even today African Americans should have a natural revulsion for decorating anything they own with large links of "chain gang" or stockade like chains, realizing and being sensitive to what most of our ancestors endured imprisoned in them. But there is a trend especially among some African Americans to decorate their license plates with large links of these type chains. They obviously see this as harmless. I view the rise of such apparent indifference or insensitivity to our past as significant.

For me it would be the same thing if Jews of our day for the sake of aesthetics began encircling their license plates with shiny decorative barbed wire or swastikas. I believe that they would be admonished severely by their community for failing to honor the memory of the Holocaust and the concentration camps that were constructed in many cases with this type fencing to assist in preventing escapes, and for failing to remember the enemy/executioners that wore the emblem of the swastika boldly as they slaughtered millions.

But there is no outcry for the Black Community as to how this is a brazen insult to our ancestors in this nation and a blatant disconnection from their suffering, suffering that some claim was so damaging and enduring they would have reparations paid to compensate. If this is so, then how can we adorn our cars with the physical symbol of their captivity and torment? It is as though we remember our ancestral anguish only when it is convenient to our present and personal agendas.

So in what ways are Black Americans going back into bondage?

****

If African Americans are truly headed back into bondage, this time it will not be the white task masters of the old south that hold us at bay. It will be the fact that we are a people without fathers. It will be because the new gods of materialism and sensuality have replaced the God of our forefathers. It will be from a lack of embracing and maximizing totally available education and educational opportunities. It will be from the inability to accept blame for our own circumstances. It will because our children are taught to solve their problems at gunpoint and that killing each other is a glamorous way to gain respect.

More specifically speaking though, our trek back into bondage will be characterized by:

1) **A lack of knowledge.** *"My people are destroyed for lack of knowledge…"* is a recognizable biblical quote from the Old Testament book of Hosea 4:6 (KJV).

   However I am not just referring to academic knowledge, which by the way at first glance appears to be on the increase. Case in point: the 2000 U.S. Census shows that the number of African-Americans over the age of 25 with high school diplomas was at 72%. This is a significant increase from the 1990 Census figure of 63% and even more highly contrasts the 1980 Census that reported this demographic at 51%. However, in working with many from this demographic I find that although they have a high school diploma their actual measurable abilities to read, spell, and perform mathematical computations are very often at grade levels far below high school. So although the number of diplomas has increased positively, I am suspect of the true amount of learning that has actually occurred.

But I am also referring to a lack of knowledge on how to achieve in our system of government and economics. It is a matter of perspective. One can assume that they are owed something and simply wait for it to come to them and complain when it does not, or one can assume that they are owed nothing and go out to make something happen for themselves and those they love. How many of that 72% with high school diplomas can tell you what system of government and economics we operate under? Or tell you anything about the bill of rights and the separation of powers. If you have no idea of what grants you your liberty and what helps you sustain it, then you are already in the process of losing it.

2) **A lack of family cohesion** – When blacks were in bondage in this nation as slaves, one of the strengths of slave owners was the ability to control the actual physical cohesion of black families, and he did so to his advantage. Since blacks were considered property not persons, owners had the right to buy and sell them as seen fit. No family was ever safe because no family member was exempt. Families could be torn apart on a whim.

While most slave owners, primarily for financial concerns I believe, appear to have avoided this with any degree of regularity, the specter of sudden and forced separation was always looming over the heads of black families. It was a part of their reality. Yet persecution often builds strength and commitment in the makeup of the persecuted. Family became that much more important to slaves. Their faith and worshiping together, eating together, struggling together, working together, all became part of what defined them and made them emotionally and spiritually cohesive at least. Made them cling harder to one another for strength; gave them a hope.

In the post *"I have a dream"* speech era, Dr. King's vision of opportunity and access has been largely realized. This is not to say that discrimination doesn't exist but that access to education at all levels is available to almost every American. Opportunity in the market places of competitive employment, business, sports/entertainment, and politics are also more prevalent than ever for all Americans. Yet African-American families are becoming less and less cohesive both physically and morally due not only to a lack of fathers being physically present in the home but also due to an ever widening acceptance of the immorality that makes out of wedlock sex and pregnancies callously acceptable. "We don't want to make the mother feel badly" is the primary reason I have heard given for this, which presents a curious paradox. If someone doesn't feel badly about negative behavior, how can the behavior be realized as bad in his or her mind? On the other hand, there is also a mixed message being sent when you tell someone that a behavior is bad but there is no consequence. All this makes it that much easier to repeat the behavior.

While there is little to no value in crushing someone emotionally and spiritually over a mistake or indiscretion, there is also no value or gain in not addressing it and calling it what it truly is. For instance, I have seen church congregations go out of their way to make young mothers (and fathers) to be feel good about the out of wedlock pregnancy and pending birth of a child. They have provided gifts, helped choose names, provided lavish christening ceremonies, and more. The emotion of healthy shame that helps us observe boundaries and or assists in repeating harmful behavior is no where to be found in this context.

I am aware that the local church is to be a place of healing and forgiveness, but I have seen both clergy and lay people alike asks the forgiveness of their congregations for moral failures, I yet to see one of those mothers or fathers offer an apology to their congregation or ask their forgiveness for behavior that runs counter to their teaching. And have rarely seen a pastor or congregation openly state that this behavior runs counter to the teaching of their own sacred text. The biggest problem here of course is that there are other young people watching all this. They see the reward, adulation, and recognition received by their peers or contemporaries. They see the acceptance without consequence for them, their child, and indirectly the behavior that brought about another fatherless or married home. So what is the logical conclusion to be expected based on their observations? We will undoubtedly see more of the same.

3) **A lack of empathy** – In the absence of empathy there is only apathy. Where is the empathy we should have for each other and our unborn? Regardless of your views on abortion, it should be apparent that its logic at this point in our history as a people is questionable. We are killing ourselves, our future. The comparatively high rates of African-American females having abortions and black on black homicides are evidence of just how little we care about our future as a people. Hispanics are now the largest minority group in this country. And while it is true that illegal immigration is probably responsible for most of this demographic explosion, they are still terminating pregnancies and killing each other far less than African-Americans. So while illegal immigration may have given them the those superior numbers, apathy among African-Americans concerning a self destruct mentality will certainly assist them in keeping this important position, that carries with it both political and economic influence, for some time to come.

4) **A lack of history** – There is a vast disconnect between where we are today as a people and the path that brought us here. Even when it comes to our original musical art forms of jazz, blues, and the spirituals they both have their roots in, these art forms which are enjoyed in most industrialized nations worldwide, are hardly ever bought or listened to by young African Americans today. Most of them that I have spoken with cannot tell you anything about pioneers like Coltrane,

Monk, Davis, Gillespie, Johnson, Muddy Waters etc. This disconnect from our artistic history as it pertains to our American culture has been substituted for such things as a knowledge of or focus on African art, which is not a bad thing but has only partial relevance to our history as a people in this nation. The African American has never existed at any other time or place in history. We are not only the sons and daughters of slaves but of slave owners. This is our country. This is our home. This is our history.

A young African American female who waited on me one night at a Dunkin Donut summed up the entirety of this historical disconnect in one question to me. She was listening to some rap rather loudly. We were the only ones in the store and so upon hearing the lyrics I struck up a conversation concerning my curiosity of how she could listen to something that said such negative things about women just because it was put to a beat. She said, **"It don't bother me."** I then asked her if she listened to any other types of music. She said "No." When I seemed surprised she asked me, "How could anybody just listen to someone sing a whole song?" - rue story.

Nothing in our societal structure aids in this problem either. The best thing that remotely addresses the issue is February, Black History Month. It is presented as a "black thing." It is not a "black thing." Black History is American History and should be presented that way. Black parents should insist on this to local school boards and textbook publishing companies. Because the first place for this information to be introduced should not be in some special month but in the textbooks that are placed into the classrooms of our students. When much of the historical contributions to this nation of its black citizens are excluded from the primary learning medium of our children, the value of those contributions remain hidden or greatly minimized. And if you were to ask many of the black students in March to tell you what they learned in February concerning the historical contributions of their ancestors to this nation, how many of them could tell you one half of the information they were exposed to in the many special event school and church programs they were exposed to? It has become as seasonal as the commercialization of Christmas. When the presents have been opened and experienced for a brief time the excitement wears off. The toys are played with less and less, and the gifts lose their sparkle. So it is with all seasonal events. Our history should be taught the school year round, and it should be American History that is comprehensive, not slanted to one segment or race. **Only when there is one history will there be one people.**

5) **Lack of spirituality** – This in no wise is a reference to church attendance, but some new reasons for church attendance and the evidence to support my opinions. African-American local congregations have always been a study in sociology. It was always one place where blacks could have a power hierarchy that was virtually unfettered from white interference. Pastors, church officers, and leading church families governed not only the local congregation but also much of this influence and adulation carried over into the greater community. Historically though their was consistently the elements of strong Gospel preaching, prayer, and a clear and expected distinction or contrast between the speech, dress code, and public conduct of those professing Christianity and those who did not. Today those lines have become blurred.

The attire and attitudes in many African American churches are today indistinguishable from the secular society they claim to serve. The church was, for the longest time, the focal point of African-American families, who for the most part belonged to Protestant Christianity.

Chapter VII
Possible Solutions

Three points to begin with. *1st: This is not a blame game.* It will not be helpful to point fingers and start reliving the past, not that the past should be forgotten. But I believe that the past can be best utilized for its value as an instrument of learning not of blame. It is in this context that we in the present can make the best use of our national, cultural, and individual histories.

2nd: There is no one in the national primetime media talking about this phenomenon or at least not in the context of it being viewed as a symptom of a greater and more pervasive issue: the disintegration of the black family structure and the seemingly voluntary trek back into servitude of the black male.

3rd: Those, the many, who shape public opinion **and supply social poisons** for the selfish purposes of their own gain will *"...not go gently into that sweet night."* **It is therefore incumbent upon us, the few, who will not turn our eyes away from the need to rise to the occasion.** There is a generation yet to be born who is counting on us, and leaving a task to someone else often means it never gets done.

****

As with every book, there are those who will read it and will plainly not get it. They will misunderstand, misconstrue, and/or simply dismiss it as much to do about nothing. If you are not in those ranks, if you do get it, then the only question is how will you respond?

If we respond with inaction it will actually make us a part of the problem. Apathy will allow most medical, psychological, or social pathology to advance. In that way, apathy actually becomes a catalyst to the disease itself. This is a vocational blight with roots embedded in and nurtured by self-defeating moral and psychosocial behaviors, behaviors that must be addressed at the individual, neighborhood, cultural, and leadership levels of our political structure.

We can pretend that it is a "black problem" or a "poor problem" and move to neighborhoods where we think we will escape that fallout. But increasingly those neighborhoods are being invaded by this fallout either through crime or other influences such as pop icons that preach or sing messages that promote these same problematic behaviors. Also unless one suffers with a degree of agoraphobia we will probably not remain prisoners in our own neighborhood forever. We and our loved ones must also venture to the outside world. There, only to be surprised by these behaviors when they inevitably meet some of us as we and our loved ones are simply coming out of a restaurant or a show, or just going to our vehicles after shopping. We are surprised because we have placated ourselves by believing that the awful things that are reported on the six o'clock news only happened to others. We have taken the ostrich approach to problem solving, believing that if we simply bury our heads in the sand the problem will go away; bad form and bad move. Even the carrying of a concealed weapon, which most people don't desire, in a situation where a criminal has the element of surprise can possibly cause more damage than to just let them have the items they are after, be that money, car, jewelry, etc.

Beginning Steps: Addressing Causality

1. **Spirituality-A light in the darkness:** I think it is evident that we have lost our way. We have for the most part lost the ability to feel empathy and need of others. It no longer bothers far too many African Americans who have achieved educationally and or economically to see the tragedy of fatherless black children roaming the streets at night when they should be safe in a bed in a home where their parents want and love them. It no longer bothers far too many young African Americans to take the lives of other blacks for whatever reason or purpose suits them at the time. The human heart left to its own devises can sink to very

low depths, petrify to unbelievable hardness, and become totally fixated on self-gratification. This is darkness of the spirit and soul of an individual and of a people. We need some light.

While this book endorses no form of organized religion, as a therapist I will tell you what I like and find good about the concept. Spirituality or religious practices in most cases, by their very nature, address egocentrism or an inordinate focus on self. Most of them emphasize something greater than self, even if it is only a collective group. Most of them also focus on placing the needs of others on the same par with or higher than your own. It gets you out of selfishness. A few pointers on this though:

- Don't send children off to religious services alone. The chances of them seeing it as a punishment and something they will opt out of at the earliest age possible increases dramatically.
- Attempt to incorporate at least some of the principles taught in your selected services into your family unit's value system and exemplify them as a parent. This will reinforce your moral authority to lead and teach, both of which are fundamental to good parenting.
- Anytime it is at all possible, especially with male children, their father (or father figure) should also attend these services with them. This increases the probability of continued attendance post mid to late adolescence and also the practical applications of that faith's basic principles in daily life. In the absence of fathers attending religious services especially their male children, the whole process maybe viewed as an activity for women and something "strong men" have no need for. Therefore the ideals that are taught in that particular faith also become at risk for being interpreted as something strictly for women or "weaklings." And if those rejected ideals are such that

promote altruism over selfishness, then it should be obvious the kind of psyche that will likely develop in the child or young person.

2. **Strengthening of traditional families:** The traditional family social unit is under assault today. And we have discussed many of the social and economic forces driving this assault. But primary to the apparent reluctance of many to race to its defense is the fact that it is not politically correct or politically expedient to do so. Instead of support there is there is angst. And proponents of the alternate family social units replacing it are generating a great deal of that angst because many of them must unavoidably and inescapably feel threatened, the reason possibly being because as long as the traditional model exists they may believe they will be viewed by many as inadequate.

In our current politically correct climate that permeates our entire society more so than global warming ever dreamt of, and where absolutes are the enemies of tolerance, it has become almost heretical to say that one thing is better than something else, or to say that one individual is better at something than another. Yet those are our truths. And they are not truths to avoid but to embrace. At the core of those truths are the spirits of competition and individualism that have made us great both economically and technologically. It is also a fact that most of those who do best in our society educationally, vocationally, and monetarily tend to come from the balance of the traditional family setting.

NASCAR has only one winner per race and one Cup winner per season. Likewise there is only one champion per season in the NFL, the NBA, Major League Baseball and all the rest of professional sports. You will not get any of these sports to dilute their championships by compromising on excellence and refusing to recognize the best among them. It would be suicide for their sport. Yet in things as important as our family units and educational systems, we have become so intent on not making anyone feel inadequate that we have redefined adequate. We no longer strive for excellence but for mediocrity. It is no longer a question of what actually "works best", in terms of real world fact and figures, but instead it is now a matter of what makes people "feel best." And while most of us are unwilling to commit to the decline of our favorite sports we are more than willing to commit to the decline and weakening of our society.

Traditional family social units work best. Why they work best is less important than the undeniable fact that they do. We should seek to bring up and nurture our children in the best proven environment possible before settling on environments that have not proven to have anywhere near the same success rates. This should not be rocket science. This should not be seen as an insult to those who did not grow up in or currently live in a traditional environment. It is simply saying that if we want to give our children the best chance at life, we should choose the best proven environment in which they are to be reared.

3. **Communities taking action and working with the sellers of advertising space:** Hopefully getting them to consider the moral and ultimate financial consequences of the promotion of seriously addicting products in neighborhoods most likely to be susceptible to becoming addicted to those products. Taxpayers will be burdened with a good deal of the costs of the health problems associated with these products. They will also be strapped with the cost of legal and penal issues that are also a part of addictive use of even a legal drug such as alcohol. Community members could also assist in trying to find alternative customers for advertisers. For instance, if a community league was organized enough, it could become a customer for the purpose of advertising what it stands for or to recruit new members. In addition, if the organization obtained non-profit status it could also be eligible to solicit for grants

and charitable donations to help with its mission of community improvement and defray some of their advertising costs. Or they could lobby for tax incentives to assist advertisers who rent space to organizations dedicated to strengthening families and communities.

4. **Tax breaks:** Establish tax incentives for Fast Food corporations and/or franchises that establish training opportunities for employees. They could also increase hourly wages as long as someone was actively enrolled in training and maintaining a passing grade. These businesses can but need not establish these training programs themselves. Why reinvent the wheel? They could partner with local colleges, junior colleges, and tech schools to enroll employees into already established accredited curriculums.

   I am aware that many fast food organizations already have management training programs. While many employees take advantage of this, as a vocational counselor, I can virtually assure you that not all employees working for them will desire careers in the food service industry given a choice. This is not a slap in the face of the industry, but it is perfectly normal that in any given pool of individuals that career interests will vary.

5. **Organized appeals to music artists:** When I was a kid in the dark ages, most of the songs by the black artists that my friends and I listened to were about love. Now most appear to be about sex, "the booty" in particular which has actually become deified for many. There was a young lady that I dated that "loved" as she put it, a particular kind of pop music… rap. It is one that I do not like because of its' constant glorification of sex, violence, and materialism in that order. I also dislike it because of the constant denigration of the female gender. In her words "It's only music. I listened to it and it didn't harm me." That was arguable. But what she was referring to was that she had a good education, a good job, "excellent credit," etc. What

146

she, like so many others whose mantra is *"it's the parents responsibility,"* failed to take into account is this; she grew up as an African American child in a middleclass two-parent household where she had boundaries and responsible role models. Most of the white children that listen to this same form of musical entertainment are in the same primary social/familial structure as was she. The children that are more negatively affected by this are the ones that come from homes devoid of such structure and balance. These lyrics and themes are literally pumped into their psyche for all or most of their waking hours. Now if you take the position that **what we listen to doesn't matter**, then I would advise you to take a quick look at Wall Street and the huge sums of capitol spent on music by which to sell products. Music registers with and conditions buyers when everything else, even sex, fails. If it is not a powerful tool for convincing, then Wall Street is throwing good money after bad each and every day of the week. I don't believe that Wall Street is that dumb or loose with its funds.

I am not attacking single parent households either. In my line of work I am acutely aware that while most mothers still are dedicated to the physical and emotional well being of their children, the number of those who are not is on the increase. Any who cannot see this, I suggest is either in gross denial or in need of an MSE (mental status exam). The children who grow up in single parent homes where the mother is more focused on her needs than those of her children are even more at risk for the negative influence of this form of "entertainment."

There is a twofold problem that exists when attempting to convince entertainers to change something about their products. *1. Most of them are rich. And many rich people (if they are honest) will tell you that their highest priority is to become even richer. 2. You also have upstarts into an industry that they have seen can deliver untold wealth almost overnight if they get the right exposure and breaks by saying and signing "the right* (or wrong) *things."* It makes the work of convincing them that they maybe complicit in the act of destroying lives even that much tougher. But we must try. It could very well mean the difference between the advancement of a culture versus its stagnation, regression, and self imposed genocide.

6. **Grant funding:** The process of obtaining grant money is often more complicated and cumbersome than the U.S. tax code and very costly in terms of dollars/man hours spent just in the preparation for the bid or application phase. And since most trained professionals usually cannot implement or start up a new human services program without financial assistance, this has the affect of scaring off many new innovative ideas and individuals. These professionals by default must then turn to existing agencies for employment and a place to practice their crafts.

The problem with this is that even though their ideas maybe fresh and untried, they are forced to work in structures that may by design force them to comply with their approaches to service delivery. The reason for this is that the majority of the management structure will probably have been around for a long time. They will have their own ideas about money, therapy, and overall agency direction. The newcomer will usually have two choices… adapt or depart.

Management may espouse verbiage that sounds very much like they embrace change and innovation. They may even believe it themselves. But the implementation of new vistas in treatment is often a long and arduous process. It requires a commitment to the long haul without abandoning the constructs of your new approach. It is totally possible to stay flexible and disciplined at the same time. It is much like a new computer program that must be debugged. You will run into problems, but you can usually fix the program without corrupting it with another

148

program or abandoning it entirely. But so often the temptation within existing agencies is to do just that. After a while, when all the excitement of the introduction of a new program with a snazzy acronym for a name dies down, the program becomes just that; an acronym. And the method of doing business becomes same old, same old.

Another byproduct of this is that no matter how well a clinician has been trained academically, within structures such as these they are almost certain to lose their skills to the point of being largely ineffective. They will probably be given success criteria for clients that reflect more of what kind of numbers juggling the agency needs to continue obtaining more funds, as opposed to just how well clients are actually doing in the long term. So in actuality the agency becomes the client and the individual in treatment only a means to an end.

All this happens because existing agencies have a history and are connected. They also tend to be a safe bet for those administering the grants. By that I mean that these repeat recipients are statistically less likely to cause them problems in the monitoring and follow-up portions of the funding. And they also know the language to use in their reports that make themselves and the grant administrators look good, which brings me to my next point.

Grant administrator positions/committees have to be more temporary than permanent. Agencies that provide services, probably by necessity in many cases, will hang on to senior staff for continuity purposes. This is understandable. But so often senior staffers dig in their heels and will not leave even when they can retire. For whatever reason they tend to stick around, and this is within their rights. But the relationships that they have established with individuals and committees that oversee grant allocations to particular states or communities cannot be dismissed as a possible factor in the distribution of funding. The actual process of writing the grant is arguably overkill and whether intentional or not, it can discourage a great many new ideas that could hold the key to some very difficult behavioral and mental health issues. When you complicate the process farther by introducing pre-established relationships, this helps no one, especially the individual in need of help.

I realize that when you are speaking about grants you are often speaking about public funds that must be accounted for. But I believe you can maintain this accountability through less complicated means. Simplicity is the key. The simpler the management structure, the less it costs to maintain and the easier it becomes to track the flow of funds, identify errors, and address needs.

Lest it is said that I am painting with a broad brush all long-standing human services agencies, let me be clear that I am not. I have worked for agencies and programs that truly did embrace innovation and change. And I still see from time to time today many of the clients that I have had the privilege of working with while employed by those agencies. The majority of them remain healthy, prosperous, and thankful for our intervention those many years ago. Some of them have approached me to thank me when I've been out with other family members who really have no real clue as to what I do for a living. Some of them have contacted me when they have heard that I was having my own difficulties to express their concerns. But agencies and programs such as these are not the rule. They are far, far too often the exception.

The Consequence of Harm: Addressing the Symptoms
It is not that responsible citizens don't see the problems of society. But rather that most of us live as prisoners of apathy that is reinforced by fear and comfort. Most of the times, unless a societal problem has direct bearing on us or those we have emotional ties

to, we place it in the category of *"not my problem."* Even when we feel as though something needs to done, we may fear for the wellbeing of self and those we love and are not willing to pay what we believe to be the probable costs of intervention. Most of us in this country have chiseled out comfortable little niches and routines and would rather not have them disturbed. We know that there can be real consequences for standing up for what is right and we fear those consequences. We fear violence and harm to those we love and ourselves. We fear the changes that might occur in our comfort zones as a result or byproduct of standing up against evil.

And yes, I believe that there is an actual force of and for evil in the world. I believe it is evil for men to hatch and abandon children leaving them to their own devices. I believe that it is evil for women to allow themselves to be used to further perpetuate this atrocity. I believe it is evil for human beings, regardless of their circumstances, to become bullies and predators feeding on and abusing the rights of their fellow human beings. I believe it is evil to turn a blind eye to all of this, deaden our own consciences with the lie that it doesn't concern us, and leave the work of addressing evil to someone, to anyone else. Sir Edmund Burke, 18th Century British statesman and philosopher said, *"The only thing necessary for evil to flourish is that good men do nothing."* To me this is more than just a well-known and often used quote. I think it is also one of life's undeniable truths.

We must find the ***core or epicenter of negative activity*** in our communities and do something. Sometimes that epicenter is static or stationary. There may be a particular house, street, or neighborhood that creates problems for those living in close proximity and as such the whole community. Remember that social sickness is much like physical sickness in that much of it is communicable. It will spread unless steps are taken to prevent this. Many of the same trends that are taking place in the young African-Americans who are the focus of most of this work are also now being reflected, to a lesser degree for the moment, in general population statistics.

Sometimes that epicenter of negative behavior may be mobile, manifesting itself in traffic, restaurants, movies, malls etc. And while no one is advocating action without regard for the safety of self and others, there is usually always something that can be done when confronted by evil even in a fluid or dynamic state. Sometimes the circumstances may allow for directly addressing individuals who are presenting as problems for themselves and others. Sometimes the situation may call for them to be addressed by the authorities or groups of concerned citizens. Each of us will have to judge this for ourselves. One thing is certain, doing nothing will only allow the problem to fester, not go away.

Keep in mind however, that what most of us will come in contact with and have the opportunity to address are only the symptoms of the greater problems. Even so we must act. For the whole idea of confronting the symptoms of social evil as may be manifested in publicly unruly, loud, dangerous, and promiscuous youths is one of care and accountability. Because most of us care about our own children, we have held them accountable for their behavior and decision making. We realize that though this can be a very tough process emotionally, in the long and short term it is meant to yield a more responsible (not perfect) child and eventually a fairly responsible adult. Someone who is less likely to engage in risky behavior, sexual or otherwise, and run afoul of the law or yield more out of wedlock pregnancies and someone who will generally be successful in life in terms of career and taxable income across their working life span.

This same care and accountability must also be reflected in society at large. We must care enough for the future of all youths that we hold them accountable to established societal boundaries. As I stated earlier, I am not advocating a willy-nilly or helter-skelter approach to any type intervention. The time to think about what we will do in any given situation is usually not in the midst of it or while in the heat of the moment. When possible, purposeful and thoughtful planning in advance is usually the better approach. Getting others to commit to action with you is good preparation. So is placing numbers for the authorities in your area on the speed dial option of your cellular phone. But the most important thing for each of us individually is to win the war within our own consciousness of *action versus apathy.*

A great deal of what has been offered to this point as "Possible Solutions" have been largely systemic (external to the individual) in nature. Before closing this section some attention should also be given to behavioral solution; those solutions inherent or internal to the individual.

Along those lines I would like to share something authored somewhere near the beginning of the last century. A black female who had very keen insight as to the needs and direction of her people in American culture authored it. Today she would be called an activist. But I think that the term would be grossly inadequate in describing the dedication she had in the cause of enlightening and empowering her people, especially black females, within the framework of the culture of her times. Yet I believe her words to also be prophetic and even more applicable in our times. Her name is Nannie Helen Burroughs.

If you are offended over the use of the word "Negro" to describe African Americans, I urge you to realize that she was using the accepted terminology of her day and I believe her work would lose something in translation if I tried to change anything. Her words speak to the temporal and spiritual parts of our existence with a gravity that cannot be denied, and with advice that is timeless.

12 Things The Negro Must Do For Himself
(Circa Early 1900's)
1. The Negro Must Learn To Put First Things First. The First

153

Things Are: Education; Development of Character Traits; A Trade and Home Ownership.

*   The Negro puts too much of his earning in clothes, in food, in show and in having what he calls "a good time." Dr. Kelly Miller said, "The Negro buys what he WANTS and begs for what he needs."

2. The Negro Must Stop Expecting God and White Folk To Do For Him What He Can Do For Himself.

*   It is the "Divine Plan" that the strong shall help the weak, but even God does not do for man what man can do for himself. The Negro will have to do exactly what Jesus told the man (in John 5:8) to do--Carry his own load--"Take up your bed and walk."

3. The Negro Must Keep Himself, His Children And His Home Clean And Make The Surroundings In Which He Lives Comfortable and Attractive.

*   He must learn to "run his community up"--not down. We can segregate by law, we integrate only by living. Civilization is not a matter of race, it is a matter of standards. Believe it or not-- some day, some race is going to outdo the Anglo-Saxon, completely. It can be the Negro race, if the Negro gets sense enough. Civilization goes up and down that way.

4. The Negro Must Learn To Dress More Appropriately For Work And For Leisure.

·   Knowing what to wear--how to wear it--when to wear it and where to wear it, are earmarks of common sense, culture and also an index to character.

5. The Negro Must Make His Religion An Everyday Practice And Not Just A Sunday-Go-To-Meeting Emotional Affair.

6. The Negro Must Highly Resolve To Wipe Out Mass Ignorance.

·   The leaders of the race must teach and inspire the masses to become eager and determined to improve mentally, morally and spiritually, and to meet the basic requirements of good citizenship.

·   We should initiate an intensive literacy campaign in America, as well as in Africa. Ignorance-- *satisfied ignorance* --is a millstone about the neck of the race. It is democracy's greatest burden.

·   Social integration is a relationship attained as a result of the cultivation of kindred social ideals, interests and standards.

·   It is a blending process that requires time, understanding and kindred purposes to achieve. Likes alone and not laws can do it.

7. The Negro Must Stop Charging His Failures Up To His "Color" And To White People's Attitude.

·   The truth of the matter is that good service and conduct will make senseless race prejudice fade like mist before the rising sun.

·   God never intended that a man's color shall be anything other than a *badge of distinction*. It is high time that all races were learning that fact. The Negro must first **QUALIFY** for whatever position he wants. Purpose, initiative, ingenuity and industry are the keys that all men use to get what they want. The Negro will have to do the same. He must make himself a workman who is too skilled not to be wanted, and too **DEPENDABLE** not to be on the job, according to promise or plan. He will never become a vital factor in industry until he learns to put into his work the vitalizing force of initiative, skill and dependability. He has gone **"RIGHTS"** mad and **"DUTY"** dumb.

8. The Negro Must Overcome His Bad Job Habits.

·   He must make a brand new reputation for himself in the world of labor. His bad job habits are absenteeism, funerals to attend, or a little business to look after. The Negro runs an off and on business. He also has a bad reputation for conduct on the job-- such as petty quarrelling with other help, incessant loud talking about nothing; loafing, carelessness, due to lack of job pride; insolence, gum chewing and--too often--liquor drinking. Just plain bad job habits!

9. He Must Improve His Conduct In Public Places.

·   Taken as a whole, he is entirely too loud and too ill-mannered.

·   There is much talk about wiping out racial segregation and also much talk about achieving integration.

·   Segregation is a physical arrangement by which people are separated in various services.

·   It is definitely up to the Negro to wipe out the apparent justification or excuse for segregation.

·   The only effective way to do it is to clean up and keep clean. By practice, cleanliness will become a habit and habit becomes character.

10. The Negro Must Learn How To Operate Business For People--Not For Negro People, Only.

·   To do business, he will have to remove all typical "earmarks," business principles; measure up to accepted standards and meet stimulating competition, graciously--in fact, he must learn to welcome competition.

11. The Average So-Called Educated Negro Will Have To Come Down Out Of The Air. He Is Too Inflated Over Nothing. He Needs An Experience Similar To The One That

Ezekiel Had--(Ezekiel 3:14-19). And He Must Do What Ezekiel Did

·   Otherwise, through indifference, as to the plight of the masses, the Negro, who thinks that he has escaped, will lose his own soul. It will do all leaders good to read Hebrew 13:3, and the first Thirty-seven Chapters of Ezekiel.

·   A race transformation itself through its own leaders and its

156

sensible "common people." A race rises on its own wings, or is held down by its own weight. True leaders are never "things apart from the people." They are the masses. They simply got to the front ahead of them. Their only business at the front is to inspire to masses by hard work and noble example and challenge them to "Come on!" Dante stated a fact when he said, "Show the people the light and they will find the way!"

· There must arise within the Negro race a leadership that is not out hunting bargains for itself. A noble example is found in the men and women of the Negro race, who, in the early days, laid down their lives for the people. Their invaluable contributions have not been appraised by the "latter-day leaders." In many cases, their names would never be recorded, among the unsung heroes of

the world, but for the fact that white friends have written them there.

"Lord, God of Hosts, Be with us yet."
· The Negro of today does not realize that, but, for these exhibits A's, that certainly show the innate possibilities of members of their own race, white people would not have been moved to make such princely investments in lives and money, as they have made, for the establishment of schools and for the on-going of the race.

12. The Negro Must Stop Forgetting His Friends.
"Remember."
· Read Deuteronomy 24:18. Deuteronomy rings the big bell of gratitude. Why? Because an ingrate is an abomination in the sight of God. God is constantly telling us that *"I the Lord thy God delivered you"* --through human instrumentalities.

· The American Negro has had and still has friends--in the North and in the South. These friends not only pray, speak, write, influence others, but make unbelievable, unpublished sacrifices and contributions for the advancement of the race--for their brothers in bonds.

· The noblest thing that the Negro can do is to so live and

labor that these benefactors will not have given in vain. The Negro must make his heart warm with gratitude, his lips sweet with thanks and his heart and mind resolute with purpose to justify the sacrifices and stand on his feet and go forward-- *"God is no respecter of persons. In every nation, he that feareth him and worketh righteousness is"* sure to win out. Get to work! That's the answer to everything that hurts us. We talk too much about nothing instead of redeeming the time by working.

R-E-M-E-M-B-E-R

· In spite of race prejudice, America is brim full of opportunities. Go after them!

Nannie Helen Burroughs

And still much remains in our present day.

Epilogue

At the end of the day, does it really matter what someone has done for a living? For those of you who still say no, may I graciously remind you that the individuals we have chosen to lead our nation and our states have been college graduates more often than not. Our mayors, congressmen and congresswomen are not usually hired from the ranks of practicing short order cooks. Rising tuition costs are a testament that it matters greatly in life and our society what one is trained to do. So as the demand for higher education billets increases, so will the cost of the billets (Econ 101).

I am not suggesting that only college graduates do well in life. We all know that is not the case. I am suggesting however that 20 year old men working in Fast Food often become 40 year old men working in the Foodservice industry or sweeping floors for a living when they could have aspired to much more challenging vocations. Now if you believe, as many do, of the young men that are just at the beginning of this journey that this is the best they are capable of, foodservice or custodial worker, then all is well with you. I am not convinced of this. I work with or have worked with the same population of men and young boys I am writing about, and I know many of them could aspire to those careers they only think about briefly in passing, convincing them self with each passing year they live that it is not something possible for them. So they live out personal and vocational lives of self-fulfilling prophecies. This cycle, without intervention, will continue.

I came from a single parent household myself. Though I had at brief intervals in my life a male figure that showed me at least in part what it meant to become a man, the rest I learned on my own through trial and error. It is not a method that I would recommend. Many don't live through it, and the ones like me who do usually bare the scars for a lifetime.

I will never discount or play down the role and influence of my mother in my life. She instilled in me my belief in God, my work ethic, proper manners, and the need for proper hygiene and education. God would later use those principles to save my life when I eventually got into serious trouble with drugs and the criminal justice system.

One of my best friend's father when we were growing up, a godly man, and one of those brief father figures in my life was a school and church custodian. I loved "Mr. John Henry." When I was around him, he treated me the same way that he treated my friend, his son. He taught us the trade working part time after school with him. It was one of our first real jobs, Gene (his son) and me. But Mr. John Henry came up in a different time. He did the best that he could with the opportunities society presented him with at the time. However, he taught my friend Gene, his seven other brothers and sisters, and from time to time myself also, to try and reach higher. He wanted more for them and I think me too. In that sense he got his dream. So I am not knocking janitors or janitorial work. I've worked in restaurants. I am not knocking foodservice or food service workers. I have never been a believer of luck. I was not raised that way. My maternal great grandmother used to say, "Luck's in the Lord and conduct's in man," a profound statement to say the least. My own personal belief is what most people refer to as luck, is merely the place where preparation and opportunity intersect. Opportunity is always happening. *Are you prepared for me?* Is the only question it asks.

Every young man that grows up without a father doesn't get into trouble with drugs or the law. But it happens far too often. And for the young black men that it happens, to one of the most common precipitation factor is that lack of a good relationship with their fathers. And I am aware that without serious scientific research on the matter this can only be stated in terms of a strong correlation. But it is a common sense correlation and remains a very good indicator for future behavior.

The Lost Boys

In "Never-Never Land" The Lost Boys never had to grow-up, food was produced through the imagination, and air travel was accomplished by just thinking happy thoughts. The treetops and caves were climate controlled and perfect for living in. And aside from the occasional encounter with an ill-tempered captain of a pirate vessel, life was good. All boys lost to hearth and homes were welcomed. What a place!

This is in stark contrast to our reality where everyone who lives long enough will grow up, at least chronologically. Where transportation is more about the cost of fossil fuel than it is about being happy, and if you want your home cooled or heated you pay your monthly utility bills or else. And if a boy or young man is lost in plain view… so what? He's not your son… right?

Emeritus

If I wished a better way
a different place from today
where what is dreamt, is what is so
to what far place would I go

would I take north and continue on
'til twilight's breath met distant dawn
where strangers never viewed my face
is that the land; is that the place

would I take west and vector 'til
stretched out flats were rolling hills
and held that route, should I then be
in my rightful home, where I was me

there is a fear that pierces deep
a strong despair and none can see
that I will never journey to
my rightful home as others do

shall someone cry, saddened for me
for glorious heights I'll never see
for perfect tastes never on my tongue
and perfect songs of youth unsung

nay; do not waste one wetted tear
on what though cherished, is never near
if you've found love, and hearth, and home
then live with joy; live long; live on.

E. Middleton

FIN